Crowdfunding
for Musicians

Laser Malena-Webber

Berklee Press

Editor in Chief: Jonathan Feist
Senior Vice President of Online Learning and Continuing Education/CEO of Berklee Online: Debbie Cavalier
Vice President of Enrollment Marketing and Management: Mike King
Vice President of Academic Strategy: Carin Nuernberg
Editorial Assistants: Emily Jones and Brittany McCorriston

ISBN: 978-0-87639-200-3

Berklee
Press

Berklee Online

Study music online at
online.berklee.edu

DISTRIBUTED BY

HAL•LEONARD
7777 W. BLUEMOUND RD. P.O. BOX
MILWAUKEE, WISCONSIN 53213

1140 Boylston Street
Boston, MA 02215-3693 USA
(617) 747-2146

Visit Berklee Press Online at
www.berkleepress.com

Visit Hal Leonard Onlin
www.halleonard.cc

Berklee Press, a publishing activity of Berklee College of Music, is a not-for-profit educational publisher.
Available proceeds from the sales of our products are contributed to the scholarship funds of the college.

CONTENTS

ACKNOWLEDGMENTS

This is my first book, and I have a lot of people to thank for its existence!

I'd like to thank everyone I interviewed for being extremely kind, generous with their time, and much more down-to-earth than "experts" seem like they should be. Thank you to sister Aubrey Turner for relentlessly believing that I could write an entire book, and for transcribing the interviews. Lucia Fasano for being the first person to allow me to give non-stop Kickstarter advice. Cary Young for teaching me how to use the Internet. Thank you to my editor, Jonathan Feist, at Berklee Press! Thank you to Doubleclicks fans and supporters for making me believe magic is real. Thanks Joseph Scrimshaw, Marian Call, Paul Sabourin, Storm DiCostanzo, Max Temkin, and Christopher Badell for offering valuable advice on crowdfunding through the years. Special thanks to Storm for reviewing the tax section.

Mom, thank you for supporting me always and never asking how this was going when you knew I was overwhelmed. Thank you, Dad, for telling me to write a book and giving lots of other great advice that I pretend to ignore. Grandpa, thank you for telling me I had to write even when I didn't feel like it. And thank you to my partner Richard Malena-Webber for being the greatest.

.

INTRODUCTION

So, you want to ask for money.

I wrote this book because I love crowdfunding. I think it's a wonderful way to make art, and it has changed my life.

In 2009, the summer between my junior and senior year in college, my sister and I started a band, the Doubleclicks. Just for fun, I picked up a guitar and learned three chords, and we wrote silly songs about video games and sang them to a patient crowd of songwriters at a local open mic.

I didn't know a lot about songwriting, or the music business, when we started. Though my family is musical, the music career never appealed to me, because it seemed full of competition, judgment, and a lot of people telling singers how to look or what to sing.

What I did know a lot about was the Internet, and that turned out to be what we needed. From the very start, our band was deeply integrated into the Internet. We posted our videos on YouTube, and were first "discovered" by fans when our song was played on a popular gaming podcast. I became obsessed with Twitter, and we befriended any fans we could find. We used online survey technology and social media to poll our fans about everything we did: where we should play shows, what kind of T-shirts we should make, how we should set up our fan club, and even what songs to play. Our fans sent in pictures of their cats to be in our music videos. We did everything together. Online.

In 2012, we launched our first crowdfunding project—not a Kickstarter, just a do-it-yourself "pre-order" for CDs, dice, and thank-yous that I built on our website with HTML and PayPal. These fans that had been a part of our whole process through the Internet supported this proto-crowdfunding experience, and that album charted at number 7 on the *Billboard* comedy chart.

Crowdfunding has been amazing for us, especially partnered with all the creative and personal connection we have with our audience. Crowdfunding allows for musicians and their audiences to have a close and wonderful relationship, and for musicians to have close creative control of their work.

Through Kickstarter and Patreon, my band has raised over $370,000 since 2015 to make albums, videos, and all kinds of cool art and products. We've done it without an agent or a manager, and we've done it while making exactly the music we wanted to make. Through crowdfunding, I found a way to make the music career work for me!

I have become an evangelist of crowdfunding and can't stop myself from talking about it. After my band had run three successful crowdfunding campaigns, I saw a friend of mine struggling. She had recorded a great album, but didn't have the resources to print or promote it. This is where my consulting business started. I used everything I'd learned about crowdfunding, about making things for the Internet, about music video production on the cheap, and about engaging audiences, to help her launch a Kickstarter. That project led to another, and another, and now I'm a crowdfunding coach on the side, in addition to being a touring musician and songwriter.

I think an online music career—a combination of touring, crowdfunding, videos, or whatever you like to make—is an extremely rewarding lifestyle for anyone who is driven to create art. It's not a shortcut or a get-rich-quick scheme, but it's a really, really rad job, and I think more people can do it than think they can, if they know where to start.

Throughout the last few years as a crowdfunding consultant, I've found myself giving the same advice over and over again, and that has brought me here: to write this book with Berklee Press. I've worked with musicians across the U.S. and internationally, genres ranging from "nerd parody" to "classical piano," "jazz singer" to "punk-rock veteran." In all of these cases, the principles for a successful campaign are basically the same, and I'm very happy to lay them all down in this book.

What This Book Is For

What is crowdfunding? It's a type of asking people for money to make something happen. Crowdfunding is not a loan, investment, or even really a "donation," but sits somewhere between those things. Simply put, several people contribute money toward a single endeavor, and in doing so, make it possible. In this book, I'll be talking about using Internet crowdfunding services to raise money for musical artists and their dreams.

This book is my instruction guide for setting off on a crowdfunding path. Whether you're just starting your musical act, or you've just left your label after a long career, this book will teach you how to prepare and run a crowdfunding campaign that respects your fans and the platform and leads to success. This book is constructed roughly in chronological order, but if you are going to use it to run your campaign, please read the whole thing before launching. You'll need to plan your endeavor from beginning to end before you start collecting money.

First, we will discuss the different types of crowdfunding tools: Kickstarter, Patreon, Indiegogo, and others. Which platform(s) should you use? What's the difference? Who is the audience for each? Let's talk about it!

In chapter 2, we'll get you started by talking about building your audience: not just how to have a lot of fans, but to have an audience that is primed and ready to back a crowdfunding campaign. Crowdfunding is a gatekeeper-free zone, which means you don't need a PR agent or label to help. But it also means you need ways to have direct contact with your fans, so we'll talk about that. This is where I give my sermon about the power of a mailing list, and I hope you are ready.

In chapter 3, I'll have you answer some important questions to set the stage for your project. The great thing about crowdfunding is that it is not a one-size-fits-all situation, and by thinking about these questions, you can frame your next steps.

Chapters 4 and 5 will introduce you to the logistical parts of a campaign, starting with goal-setting. How much money do you need to raise, and how much money *can* you raise? These are equally important questions, because you don't want to start a failing campaign, and you don't want a successful campaign that will actually lose you money. We'll also discuss the part my clients get most excited about: rewards. Everybody wants a T-shirt, a pin, a coffee cup, a tote bag, a vinyl record, and a stuffed animal with their band name on it. Let's talk about which rewards are best for your audience, and how to narrow it down so that you stay on the good side of profit and don't lose all your time writing custom songs about everybody's dogs. Then we'll combine everything: your goals, your rewards, your project, your timeline, into one big budget spreadsheet, and check all the variables to be sure that you're still in the black. That's right: it is much easier than you think to lose money on a crowdfunding campaign, even when it seems like you just made $75,000. Trust me, I've been there.

Chapter 6 is where it gets fun: we'll start designing your crowdfunding page! We get to decide how you're going to sell yourself and your project, using visuals, videos, sound, and the dreaded bio. It's time to sell yourself, and that can be uncomfortable, so let me help. Because it's about to get worse....

In chapters 7, 8, and 9, we're going to plan how you tell your friends, fans, and family about your crowdfunding campaign. Setting up a great page is nothing if no one knows about it! This is the most important part of a campaign, and it is the part where most people go wrong. This will be where I tell you how to schedule and plan promotion so it doesn't drive you or your fans crazy. You need to make these plans before you launch, so let's get to work!

In chapter 10, we go beyond just telling your fans, and tell the world about your crowdfunding campaign. This chapter will be where we talk about press placements, podcast interviews, viral videos, and other methods that bring in outside interest to your musical act and, in turn, your crowdfunding campaign. I'll include an interview with a veteran music reporter with tips on how to get coverage for your band, and some sample emails you can send to actually get a response.

Chapter 11 is where the work really begins (hilarious, right? Didn't you just do a bunch of work?), because chapter 11 picks up after you've got your money. In this chapter, we talk about fulfilling rewards, following through on stretch goals, making your album, and all the important stuff that was your plan in the first place, before you went through ten chapters just to get the dang money. Involving your fans in the process is just as important after the check has been cashed as it was before, and this chapter will include tips about that.

When the book is over, I have an appendix for you with some great resources to check out in the ever-changing world of crowdfunding.

Crowdfunding is great, and I'm very excited to take you on this journey. Whatever your passion, if you have the talent, the work ethic, and the willingness to try new things, crowdfunding is a really great way to make your art possible while deepening your relationship with fans. Let's get started!

PART I

Crowdfunding and the Online Musician

CHAPTER 1

Intro to Crowdfunding

Anybody can do it! Right?

WHAT IS CROWDFUNDING?

Crowdfunding and patronage are certainly concepts not invented by the Internet. People have been donating to make art possible for a long time, from the royal patrons who sponsored Beethoven and Handel, to passers-by throwing quarters in a guitar case.

The popular resurgence of crowdfunding in the music industry, around 2009, came at a convenient time: just about the time when services like Spotify and YouTube were becoming the way people consumed music. As these free and advertising-based services grew, album sales plummeted, and there was much hubbub about whether anyone would make money on music again. Internet crowdfunding burst onto the scene at an awesome time to help some artists find a new way to fund their art: the kindness of strangers.

Crowdfunding works like this: an artist creates a page on the Internet for their art, with their creative goals, an option to donate, and (often) rewards in exchange for donating. That artist/creator shares the project with their family, friends, and the world through social media, email, word-of-mouth, and however else they can, and then those people support the art financially.

Crowdfunding also has a large element of participation and investment, not just with money. When people pledge to help a piece of art happen, instead of just buying a CD in a store, the project becomes less of a product and more of an experience, for everybody involved. Artists need to open up their brains a little bit to let the audience see inside: the process, the decisions, or even just photos from the studio. Crowdfunding isn't a one-way street.

PROS AND CONS OF CROWDFUNDING

An online music career is not for everyone, but I do think everybody can benefit from learning about it. There are a lot of incorrect assumptions and weird notions about Kickstarter, Patreon, and other crowdfunding platforms. When you run your own career without a label or an agent, you *are* the label and the agent, so it is a lot of work. Direct interaction with fans can be exhausting and sometimes negative. Plus, it's hard to get a billboard in Times Square or a performance slot at the Grammys if you are just one person (or one band) with a modest budget for production.

However, there are a lot of benefits of a crowdfunded career that make it extremely worthwhile. You don't have to share the money you make off of your music with a label or agent if you don't have one. You don't have to take feedback from executives or committees, or worry about being "marketable" in a traditional way. You can make something very, very weird that would never "make it" in the "mainstream," and as long as there is an audience for it, you can be successful. The Internet can help create a career that is a flexible, excellent incubator for ideas—whether your goal is to eventually get signed or not.

There are also a lot of formerly signed artists who come to crowdfunding anyway! Kickstarter has hosted projects by Amanda Palmer, Mary Lambert, and Ted Leo. The now-defunct PledgeMusic platform even collaborates with labels and has hosted artists as prominent as Sara Bareilles and Lindsey Stirling. These artists have used crowdfunding to either make something in the independent style they want, or to involve their fans in a new and deep way. Crowdfunding is a wonderful way to take control of your career. It isn't a shortcut, but it is a pretty magical alternative.

Another important thing to know about crowdfunding: if you're an artist running a project alone, you are not necessarily going to get any direction. When you ask your fans for money and work with them directly, you become your own boss (and also, your fans become your boss, if you let them.) Suddenly, it's very important that you are organized and responsible. There is no one but you keeping this whole thing together. If this is a little scary to you, that's okay; in chapter 3, we will talk about the skills you'll need and how to build a team that has them.

But... what is crowdfunding? What's a "Kickstarter"? How is that different from a "Patreon"? And how do they all, actually... work? The next section will tell you about the different types of crowdfunding platforms, and hopefully give you a realistic idea of how each of them functions.

WHAT ARE THE DIFFERENT CROWDFUNDING PLATFORMS?

Kickstarter

The most well-known U.S. platform for crowdfunding is Kickstarter.

Kickstarter is a website, and a service, that allows anyone to run a fundraising campaign to create something. A creator sets a goal (say, $5,000 to record a new album), creates some "reward levels" (like $15 for a CD), and launches the project for a set period of time (usually thirty days). If enough people pledge enough money through Kickstarter's All-or-Nothing system by the deadline, the project is funded, the creator gets the money (minus some fees), and they can make their project. If that goal isn't hit, however, none of the money is collected and the creator gets nothing.

On Kickstarter, backers pledge in exchange for rewards. These are often copies of the album or creation that was funded by the project, in addition to things like exclusives, personalized or custom rewards, even concerts. Kickstarter is not just a store, but offering rewards—and fulfilling them on time—is an important part of maintaining your relationship with fans and keeping the good reputation of Kickstarter going. (Also, people can sue you if you don't follow through, so, do that.)

When Kickstarter started in 2009, it was a sort of "dream factory." If there was some wild, dream project that a creator wanted to do but could never get funded (from grants, sponsorships, a record label, or studio), they could reach out directly to the world and ask for help. In this way, new works of art, games, films, music, dance, and events could come into being that would not have had another way to exist. Creators came to Kickstarter because they believed there was an audience for their creation, but gatekeepers wouldn't let the project happen. If a project succeeded, it meant the audience existed. It's really quite beautiful.

Since that time, Kickstarter has become a lot of different things to different people. For some (especially in the board games industry), it's treated like a limited-run store or a pre-order system. For others, it's a way to build excitement about a project by getting community buy-in. Because of some anomalous huge projects (Amanda Palmer's album, the "Potato Salad" project, the card game Exploding Kittens,) some people incorrectly see Kickstarter as a way to get rich quick with minimal effort. It isn't that. Most Kickstarter projects don't make anywhere near $1 million.

I love Kickstarter, and I think it's wonderful, but it's also not a magic zone where money falls out of the sky. Creators need to treat the platform (and thus, their backers) with respect—both for their own sake and the continued success of crowdfunding in general. It's a system based on goodwill and trust, and many projects fall apart when creators forget this.

Indiegogo

Indiegogo (founded in 2008) is similar to Kickstarter, and is often seen as an alternative, though it has a slightly different approach. Indiegogo, like Kickstarter, has different levels at which backers can support. They're called "perks" instead of "rewards," and there's a set amount of time for a creator to fundraise.

The main difference with Indiegogo is that there is an option to eliminate the "all or nothing" funding threshold. If an artist sets a goal (say, $5,000 for an album) but only raises some of it (say, $1,500), they still get the money that was raised.

Patreon

Patreon (founded 2013) was cofounded by Jack Conte of the band Pomplamoose as a way to help YouTube musicians, like himself, get paid for their work beyond just the advertising revenue they got from making videos. There are tons of musicians who put out free content on the Internet, especially on YouTube, and their audiences are far more interested in those videos than they are in buying albums or even seeing live shows. However, videos don't have a tradition of being paid for, and that's where Patreon came in. Since 2013, the platform has grown beyond a place for YouTubers, to become home to comic artists, podcasters, writers, and all kinds of artists and musicians.

Patreon is an *ongoing* crowdfunding service, which means this: people pledge on an ongoing basis to support an artist. Creators can set up a project to do this one of two ways: per month, or per "creation."

For a monthly Patreon, the backers, called "patrons," will pledge a certain amount to the creator for each month. Usually, this comes with an expectation that the creator will be creating and sharing regularly with their patrons. In this way, Patreon monthly projects are a bit like subscription fan clubs that come with regular benefits for backers.

Per-creation Patronage means that patrons can pledge and will be charged each time a creator publishes a certain type of post on their Patreon page. The simplest version of this is "music video" or "song"—and in that way, Patreon provides a budget and a direct incentive for an artist to create that type of project. Some people do this with demos, with drawings, with online shows—the possibilities are endless.

Rewards on Patreon work a little differently than the "pre-order" type system that typically rules Kickstarter and Indiegogo-type campaigns. There are still reward levels depending on the amount of money pledged, but these rewards typically aren't as cut-and-dried, because the project just keeps on going into infinity (or until the artist cancels it or puts it on hold). For per-creation projects, rewards often include exclusive downloads of the song created, or chord or lyric sheets. For per-month projects, the rewards can often just be behind-the-scenes peeks, demos, or access to private channels of communication like a chatroom or video hangout.

The attitude on Patreon is a little different than other kinds of online crowdfunding. Though goodwill is a big part of any crowdfunding project, creators on Patreon tend to be a little clearer that the money they receive from their patrons is funding the mundane parts of their life: paying rent, buying supplies, basically keeping a salary. Pledgers are generally more interested in supporting the artist than getting a "product."

Personally, a large portion of my "salary" as an independent artist has come from Patreon support for a few years, and my patrons and I are very happy with that. It's a little more vulnerable and direct than buying a Kesha CD online, though in practice, it is about the same thing: a fan is using their money to help an artist survive and make more art. Have I mentioned crowdfunding is magic?

Twitch, Bandcamp, YouTube, and Other Platforms

Twitch. Twitch is a live online streaming service that started as a place to watch other people play video games, but has expanded to include talk shows, board games, and music. Some musicians have found success streaming music (or a combination of music and other types of shows) on Twitch. The platform provides a built-in donation system of "subscriptions" and "bits," which are available to creators who meet minimum requirements of hours streamed and viewers. Subscriptions allow viewers to get special features (like no ads, and new images to use in chat), and "bits" are a type of tipping. Fees are high on Twitch (they can be up to 40 or 50 percent), and it requires a lot of time investment, but the platform is a great fit for some.

Bandcamp. Bandcamp is a low-barrier-to-entry music platform, which started as a way for bands to sell their music, like an alternative to iTunes or CD Baby but with instant posting access and no submission fees. Bandcamp also provides Web streaming, merch sales, and pre-order services, which are great, and also has a "pay-what-you-want-including-free" option for selling music. Bandcamp (in 2014) launched a crowdfunding-type subscription service where fans can sign up for an annual subscription to get behind-the-scenes content like demos and videos (and whatever a creator wants to post.) It's not as widely used as Patreon, but the service is a sort of alternative or supplement to a Patreon-type service and could work well for a musical artist who wants some financial support to release lots of tracks throughout the year to their supporters, perhaps building up to an album or just to work on their skills.

YouTube. YouTube also recently added a Patreon-type donation and subscription service in 2014 where folks can subscribe to specific channels to remove ads and get special commenting options. If a band makes a lot of content on YouTube, this service is worth looking into.

GoFundMe. GoFundMe is an Indiegogo-like one-time funding platform, often used for charity or medical expense fundraisers. It can be used for music, though the broadness of scope and relatively low barrier to entry doesn't lend as much professional credibility as other platforms. People often don't expect to get something in return for a GoFundMe pledge, and it's more of a "helping out a friend in need" platform than "supporting a professional artist" one.

Other Platforms. There are many, many crowdfunding platforms popping up all the time, many of them specific to different types of projects. You'll find Seed&Spark (film), CrowdRise (non-profits), Fundly (social issues), and Fundable (startups and tech). Bandwear is a slightly different kind of crowdfunding platform: a music-focused online store creator that both prints and fulfills projects for musicians (t-shirts, CDs, etc.), and it can be set up on a band's own website or Shopify store. ArtistShare is an invite-only music-funding site that precedes Kickstarter and works a lot like IndieGoGo; it is used primarily by classical and jazz artists.

Do-It-Yourself Campaign

Of course, crowdfunding is just a concept. It was done before the Internet was created, and certainly before Kickstarter started. Many artists create their own crowdfunding campaigns to fit their needs better.

For example, comedian Jackie Kashian has a podcast called *The Dork Forest*, and simply asks her fans to donate to her every month using PayPal. Singer-songwriter Marian Call started a crowdfunding campaign called the "Donors Circle" where folks could donate online, buy music, and contribute at shows, and when they hit a minimum amount of money, they'd be added to a secret mailing list with access to behind-the-scenes information as Marian wrote her next albums and planned her projects. Nerd rapper Adam WarRock released music for free on his website all year round, then hosted an annual fundraiser every June, a bit like a public radio station.

There are donation websites like ko-fi.com and PayPal that simply ask followers to pitch in, some for a reward or access, and some just for the satisfaction of helping.

This kind of "DIY" campaign can be anything you want, and though it may require a bit more technical know-how than using an existing crowdfunding service, it can work just as well, depending on your crowd. A do-it-yourself type campaign can be great if you just have fans who want to donate for nothing in return, if you just need a small quick investment, or if your crowdfunding needs don't match up with the features provided by an existing service. Also, depending on how you do it, a DIY campaign can be cheaper than paying the fees of a crowdfunding platform.

CHOOSING A PLATFORM

Picking the right platform for your project is essential for its success. Of course, there are different answers and the platforms are adjustable. For example, musician Nataly Dawn and band the Library Bards have both found success funding albums on Patreon, where one would more typically suggest using Kickstarter or another one-time campaign for such a project.

Here are some basic things to consider when choosing a platform.

Brand Recognition/Audience and Artist Ease of Use

The brand recognition of a platform is a big one. The first time I ran a Kickstarter campaign, upwards of 30 percent of the traffic to that page came from within Kickstarter. Many, many folks who followed my band (which is a geek-centric comedy band) already had a Kickstarter account to back tech and gaming projects. Other audiences who are deeper into the music world might be more familiar with ArtistShare, while some non-U.S. audiences prefer Indiegogo because it doesn't require the use of a credit card. There is a film-specific platform called Seed&Spark that is used by a lot of filmmakers.

It's worth it to ask around and to be tuned in to your audience to find out what platforms they are most used to. If they don't have to create a new account or learn a new system, that's just one more barrier they won't have to cross to back you on day one.

Reputation and Credibility

An independent artist's ability to raise money is only as good as their credibility. There are many, many reasons to not want to lend a bass player $100. Therefore, any credibility that can be lent by a platform will be only helpful to the campaign. Through the years that crowdfunding has existed, many folks have launched projects, collected money, and never sent out rewards for one reason or another. This happens on some platforms more than others.

Kickstarter requires a "page review" and requires that projects reach a certain standard of credibility before launching, in order to fit within their rules. They have done some work on keeping errant creators on task. Indiegogo and GoFundMe have traditionally had much lower requirements, so they don't lend as much credibility as Kickstarter might. Patreon is on the newer side, and in its first few years had some problems with keeping customer data secure and making controversial fee change decisions. These are all aspects a creator should consider—and more importantly, investigate what their audience thinks.

There is also the matter of risk when deciding between an all-or-nothing service like Kickstarter and one that allows you to keep the funds no matter what, like Indiegogo or ArtistShare. If a creator launches on Indiegogo and doesn't fundraise to their goal but is still responsible for fulfilling rewards, that creator can be in deep water. For example, if you needed that $5,000 to hire a producer and print albums, what are you going to give to your backers when you only raise $1,500? You simply don't have the CDs to send them! Indiegogo is good for many specific types of projects, but because it doesn't require the big leap of faith, it doesn't exude the confidence that may translate to audience excitement and trust.

Type of Project and Timeline

What is being made? Is it an album that needs a one-time shot of investment? Is it a series of music videos, or a podcast? Or does an artist just need ongoing support so they can write music and tour? Depending on the project, this may be what informs the decision regarding what platform to use. Some artists run multiple campaigns. My band, the Doubleclicks, for example, has an ongoing Patreon campaign that pays out whenever we create a music video, but when we go into the studio, we launch a Kickstarter to cover those big one-time album costs. In the past, we also did small DIY campaigns using PayPal when we needed $1,000 or less to print a handful of CDs or a new T-shirt. It's important that the platform makes sense for your project.

Another thing to consider when choosing a platform is how long a creator has to create their project, and how soon they need the money. If a creator has a couple years before they'll be ready to produce an album, and just want to write a song a month until then, they might consider launching a Patreon where they can share rough demos with fans who pledge $1 per month. On the other hand, if the album is nearly done, the artist already has an audience, and they want to get it out the door in a couple months, an Indiegogo or Kickstarter campaign might be just the trick. If the creator needs money even sooner than that, don't have a whole month to promote something, and has a big enough crowd compared to the funds needed, a quick pre-order on Bandcamp or PayPal may provide a quick shot of cash that will help get the resources needed to release and then promote the album to the fans who don't get it on the quick campaign.

WHY DO CROWDFUNDING CAMPAIGNS SUCCEED OR FAIL?

Crowdfunding is magic when it works. Something will exist that didn't exist before, just because an audience demanded it be so and backed up their demands with money. Rad as heck. However, not every crowdfunding campaign succeeds. A lot of them don't, actually. People launch projects on Kickstarter and Indiegogo every day that get no backers, or not enough to get funded. It's sad. How can this be prevented? What does a project need to succeed?

Talent, Taste, and an Awesome Product

Artistic talent is one thing this book can't help you with, unfortunately. There are a few mysterious qualities as to what makes someone a musician people listen to versus a musician nobody wants to hear. Talent, skill, good taste in knowing what to produce—those are absolutely necessary. Not just everyone can sell just any album or song. It has to be something that some people will like. It doesn't have to be for everybody, but it has to be some minimum level of "good." If an artist isn't "good" yet, if nobody (except your mom, sometimes) listens to them, then perhaps practice and training will help—or perhaps not. Maybe you need to try a new genre, or find a new approach. There are some people who work very, very hard and do not "make it." This may seem obvious, but it's not. Sorry, buds. It's just true.

An Existing Audience Who Has Money and Goodwill

You need people to raise money. You've gotta have a crowd to crowdfund! We'll dedicate chapter 2 to helping create that audience, but this is something that takes time. Most people who are *very* successful on crowdfunding don't just start by creating an $80,000 Kickstarter. Often, these are people who have spent years honing their craft, sharing art for free online, and gradually building an audience. Some of the most successful campaigns are excellent demonstrations of this. Exploding Kittens, the most-funded campaign in Kickstarter history, was the third crowdfunding campaign created by Matthew Inman, a cartoonist who had been, prior to that campaign, putting up comics for free on the Internet for six years. Amanda Palmer, who created the biggest music campaigns to date on both Kickstarter and Patreon, spent twelve years building a crowd through her band the Dresden Dolls and her solo act. Not only had she been signed to a label, she also built up a huge independent audience through touring and providing nearly all of her music as free downloads on her website.

To be successful with crowdfunding, a creator certainly doesn't need to have an audience or career the size or length of those examples. But they do need an audience, and they need to balance that audience with their expectations and a realistic goal.

Realistic Goal

If the Beatles all came back to life and launched a Patreon page tomorrow, they might be able to make it to the moon. I don't think Aimee Mann could do that, but she could make a great album for $100,000. If a band has 200 dedicated followers, they may not be able to go into the studio for a $20,000 rock-produced album, but they can likely make something for $2,000—maybe a killer intro EP? Anyone with friends can have a successful campaign, if their goal is realistic. It's also possible to build up through a series of campaigns to that big project, with wise use of crowdfunded money and time.

Unrealistic goals are the leading cause of failed campaigns, in my experience.

Skills and Time

Running a crowdfunding campaign is a lot of work. It is not a bug trap or a light switch. It's something you need to babysit, to work on, to write about, to promote. It also requires a whole bunch of skills aside from the creation of music—especially communication skills and professionalism. And you can't just be smart; you have to be smart *and* willing and able to dedicate time to your project. Folks have said that running a Kickstarter is a full-time job, and that can certainly be true. For the months surrounding a project, you will need to dedicate a lot of hours to preparing, promoting, and fulfilling your project. And if you don't? It just won't be as successful. You'll get out of crowdfunding what you put into it. It is not a shortcut.

The Right Mindset

Crowdfunding can be a bit of a mystery to folks who haven't done it before. From the outside, it can look like a get-rich-quick scheme. It's not, I promise. Even people who raise a lot of money don't actually get to keep most of it. They're using that to make art. But that's the whole point. It's a magical thing, if your goal is to create art. It's a bit of a disappointment if you're just trying to get rich.

CHAPTER 2

Building a Crowd on Social Media

Because to "crowdfund," you need a "crowd."

When a client approaches me to run a crowdfunding campaign for them, the very first questions I ask are these: Who is your audience, where are they, how do you communicate with them, and how many of them are there?

If this quality audience doesn't exist (yet), we can't start asking for money. There is a misconception that Kickstarter and Patreon are just websites where money comes from. That's not it. The money comes from people—mostly, people who already know the music. The crowdfunding platforms are just the conduits to connect creators and audiences together. Crowdfunding can help build momentum for an audience to grow, of course, but that comes later. Artists need to have an engaged, active, and invested online audience before they even start the process of crowdfunding.

Be ready to spend some time building an audience. If you don't have an audience at all, you're going to need to spend some time on getting your numbers up. And it may take you a while, too, to hone your art and your online personality to be something that people like. Developing a following is a skill.

This is not to say all artists need to spend all of their time on social media building an audience. Mostly, I think an artist should do what feels right and brings them joy. But from a pragmatic perspective, if a creator's goal is to raise money for music using crowdfunding, they need a group of people who are willing to give them money. That means you need fans that have spent enough time with you, online or in-person, that they are willing to back you for no other reason than joy and pride. Music is basically free these days, because of Spotify and YouTube. Value is added through emotional connection with an artist, or the excitement of participation.

As a musician, you are selling much more than a product. You're selling a connection and a feeling of support, and people want to feel that with someone they already know and love.

To become a part of someone's life and create this connection, artists can do a few things. Firstly, of course, an audience needs access to that music, perhaps through a free EP or an active YouTube channel. Secondly, they need some connection: artists can bring fans into the fold with personality filled Instagram stories of tours and shows, through weekly art, or daily mantras. There are a lot of ways to build an audience, and we'll give lots of examples in this chapter.

All that is to say this: before you launch a crowdfunding project, your audience needs to exist, and that's why this chapter is going to be all about how to create a deep connection with your audience!

There are three important goals for creators to keep in mind when grooming an audience for a crowdfunding project: quantity, investment, and access. A brief overview:

Quantity. This is the easy one: Ideally, an audience as big as possible.

Access. So, a band has a huge audience. That's wonderful! But there's one more essential pillar to this crowdfunding success structure: that band needs to be able to get in touch with them immediately.

A huge audience who only sees their favorite band at live concerts or when they post a new song on Spotify won't know when that band's crowdfunding page launches, and there is a limited time to build momentum for success, especially on limited-time platforms like Kickstarter. This is where mailing lists, social media, and a marketing plan come in. Artists need to know how to contact their audiences in a way that they like and expect.

Investment. A big audience isn't anything, though, if they aren't honestly interested in the art that's being created. I have many times seen bands with enormous numbers of views on YouTube or followers on Instagram who have a hard time translating those people into crowdfunding backers. Sometimes, this is because the relationship is casual, or because the backers think of the artists more as TV stars and less as people who need their support to create art.

One specific instance of this is a friend of mine who makes two kinds of YouTube videos: covers of popular songs and original music. She has a huge audience for her cover videos, but the original music doesn't attract that audience. Therefore, when trying to crowdfund new original music, that quantity just doesn't translate to money.

It's important for creators to create an audience that is connected with both the artist and the art they want to make. Even if view counts are lower, having a quality connection with an audience can translate to a bigger crowdfunding result. This can be achieved through honesty, intimacy, and going to the points of low competition. We'll talk about all of that later in this chapter.

Every musical act starts at a different level when they begin a crowdfunding project, so I'll be explaining the "audience building" process by taking three different examples of fictional artists—Marieve, Barry Barrowman & the Bigtime Band, and Ghoul Gang—who have different strengths and weaknesses. Every act could do some work to boost their online audience and their connection; there's always room for improvement. Of course, most creators don't necessarily need to do any work to build their audiences before launching their projects. They will simply make less money.

These ideas will help your band bring in listeners who eventually become fans, and then backers or "customers." It's not a romantic concept, but by building this groundwork, a musical artist can create a "sales funnel"—a pathway that subtly but inevitably leads the new fan to support the art financially.

The following strategies are low-cost (compared to hiring a promoter or PR firm or having the help of a record label) but require time investment and some strategic thinking. Mix and match these ideas and suggestions to help your act get more quantity, investment, and access in your audience.

QUANTITY

Marieve is a classical pianist. She just finished graduate school in music with a huge catalog of compositions (on her hard drive) and lots of talent and skill. Her friends and family come to her recitals, and everyone agrees that she's incredible. She wants to record her debut album and go on a tour, so she looks to set up a crowdfunding campaign to pay for all of that. But... where to begin? Marieve spent all her time in school working on the music, not marketing it or posting on Instagram. So, her fan base just consists of her personal friends and people who saw her at events over the last few years. Where is her money going to come from?

How does she begin the process of developing a sustaining fan base?

First of all, if Marieve wanted to Kickstart a basic, $500 EP with just the help of her friends and family, I bet she could. Anybody can have a successful Kickstarter if they ask for a small enough amount of money—and we will talk about realistic goal-setting in chapter 4. However, Marieve wants to launch her indie career, and I'm here for her. Let's get started.

Get Ready to Be Discovered

First of all, Marieve needs to create accounts for her music on all of the social media. Instagram, Twitter, Facebook, and YouTube are the current big ones, but she should also talk to her friends and see what everyone is using; the landscape changes quickly. Even if a creator doesn't read or post on social media frequently, their musical act should still be present. That way, when the act appears on a bill or meets someone in real life, it's easy for an audience or new acquaintance to "tag" and follow that artist on their platform of choice.

Don't make it difficult for someone to be your fan. It's part of an artist's job to be easy to find.

Marieve should also update her social media regularly. If this doesn't come naturally, she'll need to take some time to read and learn. Take a look at "Different Platforms, Different Posts," (page 38) to see some good examples of updates and how frequently to post.

Marieve also needs a website, somewhere to collect all of her links and share her music, post news, and display concert dates. That may seem basic, but it's important. A good website should also have a great bio and high-resolution photos that could be used by blogs or newspapers. We'll talk more about building a great press kit in chapter 10.

All of these accounts should be easy to find and easily linked to one another. There should be an easy way to access every social media page from Marieve's website, and an easy way to get to Marieve's website from her social media. There should be one-click solutions to "listen to new music" and "follow" on any platform. It should be so, so, easy for a new listener to make Marieve's music a part of their life.

Get Discovered

Once Marieve has done the basics of "being ready to be discovered," she needs to create more content. "Content" is an Internet-person way to say "music, videos, photos, blog posts, and anything else that people can consume online."

I would tell Marieve at this point to launch some sort of self-directed project, with a name, involving her music. This could be anything, so let's give her some guidelines.

The trick here is to create content that will get an artist discovered by lots of people, but not just *any* people: people who will want to support that artist in creating the music they want to create. So yes, one could perform beautifully sung a capella covers of Disney songs and perhaps reach a million views, but if that person's true passion is a career performing original folk music, they might not want to find their audience that way.

There are so many things musicians can create and upload to the Internet, and there are ranges on every axis:

- covers of popular songs, or original songs
- high-quality, big-budget music videos, or videos you made with a cell phone or computer webcam
- a full-length, mastered album, or a demo recorded by one person in a closet

There are cases to be made for all of these types of media, but the expense shouldn't be what an artist focuses on. In my experience, online audiences (the good ones) care about honesty, talent, and consistency. They care much less about how much money was spent on a project.

- **Honesty.** If you're reading this book, my hope is that you want to make good, honest, art. Crowdfunding isn't where somebody goes to "sell out." Crowdfunding and independent online music is intimate and borderless—and that's what makes it brilliant. So, make the music you want to make, and make "content" that you are proud of. Don't worry about what other people, especially people who are already popular or have the backing of a big label, are making. When you start with a small audience and a small career, your art can be small too.

- **Talent.** If you are an inspired writer of lyrics, you don't need a $50,000 music video production inside of a volcano. If you're amazing at guitar, just play your guitar.

  This is also an important point to take stock of all of your skills, especially the ones outside of music. Some people want to dabble in camera work or filmmaking—obviously that's a wonderfully symbiotic partner to an online music career. But if that's not you, there are still a bunch of things you can do. If you draw, make a time-lapse drawing video for your song. If you foster cats, use them in your videos. (Look up Sarah Donner for amazing use of cats in a music career.) If your career is in computers, or journalism, graphic design, or maybe you're great at video games—take those other aspects of yourself, and use them to create art. Make the thing that only you can make.

- **Consistency and a Name.** People like knowing what to expect, and the Internet is full of chaos. I've found that a project with a schedule and a name has a much better chance of "catching on" than something without a consistent concept behind it.

That "name" thing is huge. Use your project's name for a concert series, a video series, and of course an album. When something has a name, it seems like a "real thing" that people can talk about. Plus, it's a built-in hashtag! Here are some ideas with a consistent schedule and name that I've seen work:

- "Weekly Song Wednesday," a new music video, every week, on YouTube.

- #littlecoversongs. Using an "a capella" app, a 15-second cover video posted to Instagram, complete with hashtag.

- Monthly, weekly, or even daily online shows (with a name like "This Band Live!") on YouTube, Twitch, or another live-streaming platform. Take requests, or don't!

- "Covered with Kittens." Sarah Donner, as mentioned, is a musician who fosters cats, and she covers songs while cats are crawling all over her. It's very good.

- "Bedhead Music Series." Juliana Finch records a song in the morning before she's showered or put on makeup.

Consistency is good not just in timing, but also quality. I would much rather see a low-fi project done well than a high-res project done poorly. (Just like I'd rather see someone play a simple version of "Twinkle, Twinkle, Little Star" very well than an impressive Bach etude with starts and stops and wrong notes.) Figure out what you can execute successfully and do that, it will be much more watchable.

Regularly and frequently updating with new content—something new for the audience to enjoy—will also make an artist a part of their fans' routine, and thus their identity. If I know that I'm going to spend my lunch break every Tuesday watching a new video from my favorite band, that band becomes part of my routine, and a part of my life. I can be thankful for that, I can share that with my friends, and I will be excited to know how I can support that in the future. I want a shirt of that band, because I spend lots of time with them. The more frequently an artist is part of their fans' day-to-day, the more that fan wants to be an active member of the artist's community, too.

So, given all of that information, I would coach Marieve to start her own project: something that is sharable on social media that has a hook and that appeals to her own taste and interests. The art part of it should definitely come from the heart, but the delivery mechanism should appeal to the Internet; the Internet loves video, it loves *short* videos, and it loves consistency.

Marieve has no video skills, but she has an iPhone and a piano by the window, so she decides to take suggestions of "moods" from her fans and posts a new video every Monday where she makes up a 20-second song. It's an interactive project within her abilities, and it's got a name: "Moody Marieve Monday." She posts this on Instagram, Facebook, and Twitter every week, and puts them all together into a big YouTube video at the end of each month. Her fans come to expect the project, and new fans are enticed by the ability to participate. Bonus: she now has content on her social media pages, and a website full of links to new things.

WHAT IS A HASHTAG?

A *hashtag* is a tool used on social networks (like Twitter and Instagram) to help people connect various posts and projects together by theme or content. They're frequently used at events and concerts; an organizer of the event Ghoul Party might ask people to "tag" their posts with a hashtag "ghoulparty2020", which means they'd include the text "#ghoulparty2020" in the caption of their Instagram photo or Twitter post. Organizers, attendees, and anyone who sees that post can click on the hashtag to visit other posts with the same tag, even by other people.

Hashtags are also used in more broad collections of things: #catsofinstagram is a popular tag, for example, or #womenwhorock. A hashtag can also be a helpful way for a single creator to group posts about a single project together like a tour, series of videos, Kickstarter project, or an album. If a band uses a hashtag to post photos in the process of creating an album—from songwriting, recording, and crowdfunding to performing—a fan could then use that one hashtag to see the entire history of the project, and even use that hashtag when posting their review of the project.

Finding Fans in Unexpected Places:
Go to the Point of Low Competition

There's a lot going on, on the Internet. There are a lot of bands. So, what makes a band unique? That's the trick.

My band performed at a popular open mic in Portland, Oregon every week when we were starting out, and met a lot of musician friends this way. But there was one weirdo who always showed up, a comedian who did five minutes of stand-up at a *very* musician-specific open mic. He didn't fit in at all, and it was strange that he was there. But whenever we or anybody needed a comedian to perform at or host an event, he was the guy we went to! He was the only stand-up comedian we knew.

Get yourself in similar situations. Figure out where your potential fans might be hanging out, and go there. What are the qualities of your music, beyond the "music" part? Do you talk about depression? Are you obsessed with flowers? Do you talk about the local landscape? Do you have a song about your favorite TV show or animal? Does your latest music video have a bunch of Pokémon in it? These are great things to think about so you can "go to the point of low competition"—that is, be the only band in the room.

Then, look for Facebook groups and post your videos. Check out reddit.com and see if there's a place to post a video in a specific category (like your neighborhood or a fan subreddit for a specific event). Submit your band to perform at festivals that don't usually have music but share other interests. The Doubleclicks, for example, have opened for authors, played at craft fairs, even performed in the intermission of a costume contest at a sci-fi convention.

It takes a lot of courage to bring your act somewhere that acts like yours don't usually go. Some people might be weirded out by your music, and some folks might insult you for "self-promoting." That's okay. As long as you're being polite, following community rules, and you're listening as much as you're talking, you can't really be blamed for trying. You don't need to defend yourself and you don't need to fight. It may be intimidating, and you may not find dozens of fans from each thing you try, but you may find a handful that you simply wouldn't have found otherwise, and that's great! Reaching out to online communities like this is like hanging up posters all around town, except with more efficiency.

A bonus benefit of reaching out to nonmusical communities is that you'll have a unique audience. When someone puts on a local songwriter night, you can bring a whole bunch of people who have never been to such a show! You're suddenly a resource and a conduit to an untapped market. It's pretty awesome.

Make Friends

Crowdfunding: you *did* come here to make friends. Crowdfunding is a wonderful example of "a rising tide lifts all boats." If you want to get an audience (and money!) from the Internet, it's beneficial to find a group of peers who are doing the same. These are the people who can share advice, who can spread the word about your shows and projects, who can open for you on tour (and vice versa). Having a community is essential, and you'll need them when we get to chapter 9!

When Marieve got out of school, she had no friends other than her classmates (who are valuable friends!). She'll start by following her heroes and her friends on all her social media and becoming an active fan of their work. And then she'll find new friends!

It can feel isolating to try to make friends, or even find new music, on the Internet. It's possible to find, connect, and then collaborate with other artists across the world by being genuine and generous!

Find: There are lots of ways to discover other acts with whom you can commune and share an audience. Go to live concerts and open mics. Ask your fans what bands they listen to. Check out hashtags, search on YouTube, and read blogs. To be an online product, you need to be an online consumer, too, so don't be selfish with your time. Look beyond music, as well. Some of the most supportive artist friends I have are authors, visual artists, and animators. We all enjoy each other's art and share it with our followers, thus building a great community of collaboration that's much more interesting than a list of similar bands.

Connect: I can't tell you the number of times I have picked a guest artist or opener just because they've been an active fan of my band on the Internet. Everybody wants positive feedback, and you can provide it. Artists are well-positioned to be the best possible fans, because you know what people like you want to hear. So, build up your karma and make friends. It will benefit you, but you should do it because you honestly like these people and their music. Comment on YouTube videos, retweet big announcements, and back people on Patreon. Create a Facebook group for local musicians or people who do the same thing as you. Beatles covers, harp playing, EDM—whatever it is, make a community! Independent artists especially need to connect with each other, because we're all making it up as we go along. Find your people and help them. Be an active and generous fan.

Collaborate and Listen: When you share someone else's music with your fans, you aren't losing fans; you are becoming a resource where they can find new music. So, collaborate with your new musician community. Make videos together, do shows together, create fundraisers together for charities you all support. My band started a monthly online show, and we have a different special guest musician every month. Get and give gigs, and create new things. Making friends should be a huge part of your music career.

Marieve browses Instagram hashtags until she finds one specific to the brand of keyboard she owns. Weird, right? But great! The #YamahaP45 hashtag is full of other musicians who are making a variety of types of music and trying to "make it." Marieve comments on posts and eventually gets followed back by a handful of other composers, all around the same level of "fame" (number of Instagram followers) as her. She shares their compositions, buys their albums, and generally is a supportive friend, and they do the same for her. She starts a Facebook group where they can share composition software tips and piano memes. Eventually, when one of these new buddies is touring through her town, they ask her to open for her at their gig.

ACCESS

Barry Barrowman & the Bigtime Band have gigs up and down the East Coast every weekend. They play coffeehouses, festivals, and local events. Whenever somebody sees them, they want to book them. The Bigtime Band is on Twitter and such, but really their audience is only at the shows. Fans see a Bigtime Band gig posted in the paper, and they show up. Well, now the Band wants to start getting serious, devote more of their time to music, and stop using their own money from their day jobs to pay for recording songs and making music videos. However, if they launched a Patreon project tomorrow, the Band's audience wouldn't know until they were on tour again. What do they do?

The Mailing List

Someday, I'm going to be wearing a sandwich board in the middle of a street somewhere, and the sign is going to read: MAKE A MAILING LIST AND TELL PEOPLE ABOUT IT. I love my email list, and I love sending my fans newsletters using that list. I love it. I need it.

The mailing list/email list is a communication tool your band can use to directly contact fans. Using an online form or a piece of paper at your show, you can gather your fans' email addresses, and then send out a newsletter (or "email blast") to those fans whenever you want. Keep reading for some guidelines.

The email list is a strange thing in 2019. A few years ago, it seemed like social media was overtaking instant messaging, message boards, websites, and email as ways to communicate online. However, now that social media is splintering and people are weaning themselves off the addiction, it seems like email may again be the only way to reliably contact some folks on the Internet.

Email lists account for a plurality (usually up to 40 percent) of the funding for my band's Kickstarter campaigns, and those of my most successful clients. Email lists get our fans out to shows and keep them updated on our latest videos. Even when fans quit Facebook or go on vacation, the email newsletter will still hit their inboxes.

It may not work for every customer, but to me, a mailing list is also a must-have for a "definitive" version of your band's news. If you want people to know it, send it in an email.

I want Barry Barrowman & the Bigtime Band to have an email list, and to send an email to that list every month with news, upcoming gigs, and a link to a free download of a song.

There are services online to set up a mailing list like MailChimp and FanBridge. Those work well, but they cost money. If an artist doesn't want to pay at first, they can boot up a free service like Google Forms, add a link on their website, and put out a piece of paper at shows. All those email addresses can be added to a spreadsheet (like a free Google Sheet), and artists can just send out a big bcc'd email newsletter that way. Once a list gets to 200 people, the artist will probably need to pay for a real service so the message doesn't get sent to spam filters.

What I really need Barry to do is start a mailing list, and start it now.

Writing a Good E-Newsletter

A mailing list (a list of email addresses) is vital to my band's success, and it works extremely well as a communication tool for artists of all genres. An e-newsletter is an email message (sometimes called an "email blast") that you send to your whole mailing list — you probably get a bunch of these from clothing stores, brands, apps, and anyone else who manages to get your email address. Of course, getting a lot of emails can be annoying, but chances are, some of your fans would love to hear what you're up to. A great e-newsletter, used correctly, is an excellent way to keep in touch with your fans.

1. **Give incentives to sign up for the list and to open the message.**
   For example, my band offers a link to download one of our old songs for free in every newsletter we send out, and we publicize that on the sign-up page we put out at shows. We also ask folks to give us their zip codes when they sign up, and we use that information when planning tours and sending targeted email blasts. Newsletter sites like FanBridge will allow you to search through this geographical data. At a concert, we'll say, "If you want us to come back to your town, cast your vote by signing up for our email newsletter at the merch table!" This works surprisingly well.

2. **Be polite with your frequency.** The more newsletters a musical artist sends out, the more likely they are sending "too much news," which is just going to annoy people, who will then unsubscribe. Artists should limit themselves to the "big stuff," and send something to your mailing list just when you need to. I like to keep it to once per month or less often, but different frequencies will work for different communities. Don't beg your audience for votes for ten online contests a year, don't send an email to the whole world just to announce that you have a gig in Duluth. Either save up that news until there's going to be something for everyone in the newsletter, or gather and use geographical data, if you have it, to only send out last-minute show notifications to people who live in the right city for it. Don't fill a newsletter with reasons to unsubscribe. The message should have something for everyone who opens it.

3. **Be visual, concise, and easy to skim.** Make a plan for your newsletter, and separate it into sections: a new video, a crowdfunding or news announcement, and tour dates, for example. Use subtitles and images to break up the message, but don't make it too long, and don't put anything in there just to take up space. Keep in mind that by percentage, most people aren't going to open your email, and if they do, they probably won't want to read the whole thing, so put your big news up top and don't bury anything big too deep into a paragraph.

4. **Provide one-click and no-click information.** Pepper newsletters with all the relevant links your reader will need, and make them easy to find and click. Tickets links, Facebook posts, your Patreon link—it should all be right in there. Fans shouldn't need to take more than one step to follow up on any information they read about. When possible, provide all available information in the email. Don't just say "tour upcoming." Instead, write "New York City, Saturday October 10." Fans don't have a lot of time, and there's a lot to look at on the Internet, so artists benefit from having a newsletter that is quick to read.

5. Be positive! One great way to make people want to open your newsletter is if they know that doing so will make them feel good. Share your successes, say thank you, and include photos of recent tours and fun things in your career. A bonus: if someone sees the behind-the-scenes of every step of your way, they'll be invested in your success and want to continue to be a part of it. Give 'em something to brag about.

SAMPLE E-NEWSLETTER EMAIL MESSAGE

Subject Line: New Ghoul Gang Song and West Coast Shows!
Hello, incorporeal pal!

Happy mid-January 2020, everyone! Life comes at you fast, eh? We're deep in the midst of planning for recording our next album and can't wait to share it with you through a Kickstarter very soon!

Coming up in the next few weeks, we have concerts coming up in California, Washington, and Oregon! Can't wait to see you.

We also have a brand-new single out on our YouTube channel (link). It's all about that feeling when you realize you've been secretly dead for years but you still love your friends!

Upcoming Shows
View our full show calendar at **ghoulgangmusic.com/shows** (link)

1/24 - Los Angeles, CA at the Stench: 8 p.m. (tickets)
1/25 - Fresno, CA at the Eccentric Chipmunk: 7 p.m. (tickets)
1/26 - San Francisco, CA at Keyboard Battle: 9 p.m. (tickets)
1/28 - Eugene, OR at The Duck's Big Choice: 9 p.m. (tickets)
1/29 - Portland, OR at Theater of the Siren: 8 p.m. with the PDX Boards (tickets)
1/30 - Seattle, WA at Way-out Coffee (tickets)
1/31 - Vancouver, WA at Sharon's Place (tickets)

As always, you get a free download for reading this far! Click here to download our 2008 song "I'm Just Extremely in Love with my Body" (link)

We will see you all soon!
Xoxo Ghoul Gang

Social Media for Live Audiences

Transferring an audience from a live event to the Internet (and vice versa) can be tricky, but it's vital. To have a successful online crowdfunding campaign, an artist will need their real-life audience to be following them on the Internet, not just so that they can hear about the project, but also so that the music and the band is part of their day-to-day lives and their identities—so important that it's worth spending money on.

Here are some effective tricks to get live audiences to follow a band on the Internet.

1. **Make video-recordings at live shows, and post or stream them online.** Share the special ones: highlights, songs, or full shows, and talk about it at your show. Fans who want to relive the fun moment or share it with their friends will seek out the recording to remember "being a part of it." It's a good idea to let your audience know that you're filming when you do this!

2. **Take a photo of your audience,** or a selfie with your audience, during your show (with permission!), and tell the crowd you'll be posting it and where (on Facebook, Instagram, etc.). People love photos of themselves and will go to check it out. If your page looks good, they'll follow you while they're there!

3. **Use your social media while on tour to post pictures of local sights and experiences.** Ask for food recommendations and take photos at popular spots! Many a time, I have kept a vigilant eye on a bands' social media before they play in my town, because I want to have shared experiences with them or see if we might run into each other somewhere. You can also mention during your show this social media experience, for example: "We ate an enormous Chicago pizza today and posted a pic on Instagram, check it out!" Or "Please tweet us suggestions of where we should have brunch tomorrow."

4. **Ask your fans to post videos/photos from the show, and then like/share them.** The more specific this "ask" is, the better. This is what my band does: "Please post pictures of us on Twitter and tag us @thedoubleclicks. My mom just learned how to use Twitter, and she loves seeing them!"

INVESTMENT

Ghoul Gang are "Web celebrities." They have made a couple spooky punk-rock videos that have gone "viral," and have over 100,000 views. Their videos have been posted on popular blogs and even played on TV! The videos are high-quality because some friends of the band were in film school and offered to help make them. However, the band doesn't make money on those videos, and they can't find people— even in their hometown—to come out to shows. Some people watch their videos over and over again, and some have subscribed on YouTube, but Ghoul Gang doesn't have the funds to record an album. They don't just want to make occasional music videos online; they want to tour and record!

Ghoul Gang needs to make an invested audience out of a large one. These are my suggestions, primarily involving turning Ghoul Gang from an amusing three-minute experience (one video) to a deep well of content that people can spend ten to twenty minutes per week enjoying. When listeners spend more time with an artist, that artist becomes a part of their identity, and they turn into fans—or even superfans!

Create an Internet Hole

One of the best ways to turn a casual fan into an "invested" one is to spend time with them—or at least, to allow them to spend time with the music. When a new listener first discovers a band's music, they will become more invested earlier if they can "fall down a hole" with that music—if they can spend a few hours glued to their computer, ignoring other responsibilities, and getting to know this new act.

Before creating this content, artists should make sure to follow the rules from "getting ready to be discovered" earlier in this chapter. Remember, every new piece of content should have links to check out the music, and fans must be able to follow the artist on all the social media, and join the mailing list, with good provided reasons to follow. Maybe a viewer won't click on a "join the mailing list link" the first time they see an artist's most popular video, but if they keep seeing that link as they watch more and more videos, eventually they'll want to join in.

Sure, not everyone is going to fall down the hole. Some people just want to watch Ghoul Gang's cover of "Call Me Maybe." But not every casual fan has to be a deep fan. If Ghoul Gang's popular videos have 100,000 views, and their little no-budget demo video for a new song only has 150, that's okay. Those 150 dedicated fans can fund a $6,000 Kickstarter, whereas 100,000 casual fans don't fund anything. Catering to superfans is how a band gets more superfans, who will follow every move and support crowdfunding projects!

Free Content

How do you make this Internet hole? Create content! So much content! Artists can make new stuff (videos, songs, etc.), of course, but they can also find and use the content they already have. If they're rehearsing, they can make a video. If there's a song written, why not make a quick, low-quality video of it? If an artist is taking pictures from the van on tour, why not turn that camera around and make a little video diary? There are lots of options on how to fill up a YouTube page or Instagram. I recommend that bands pick the ones that seem fun and fit the personality of the art.

Here are examples of free content that bands can make.

1. Homemade song demos

2. Homemade music videos

3. Lyric videos for other songs you've already posted

4. Video blogs of the band on tour

5. Long videos: Did someone tape a concert? Did you livestream a video game on Twitch? All of that is great, long, free content.

6. Blog posts about touring on the band website, with photos

7. Jokes on Twitter

8. Pictures of dogs on Instagram

9. Songs available to stream on Spotify. Yes, release an EP of demos! Do something wild!

Incentivize Participation

Ghoul Gang has a lot of viewers, but not a lot of participants—that is, people who are commenting, following, and supporting. It's easier than one might think to create new ways to get people to participate!

- **Incentives.** Give out some free digital music! The website Bandcamp will let fans download music for free, and an artist can require that to do so, the fan must sign up for an email list. How great is that? Everybody loves free stuff, and this "give out a free single"—or even a free cover song—has been a great tool for many of my clients to build up their email lists. It doesn't have to be a studio-quality recording. After all, it's free!

- **Community.** Comment sections on YouTube and Instagram are great evidence; fans can enjoy talking to each other. Chances are, fans of a certain musical act have more in common than just that one album. Make a place for your fans to meet each other. This could be a Facebook group, a message board, or a chatroom using the Discord service. A comments section is a place where fans can talk about the things they like: their pets, their other favorite bands, their goals and dreams. Hopefully, they can make friends, or maybe even make things together! Lots of people meet through fan groups like this, then meet up at shows, and create long-lasting friendships. If a band is a way somebody finds new friends, they'll appreciate it. Bonus: this is a place a band can go to share important news with the most dedicated of fans.

  A note on groups: it's a good idea to set rules for communities like this so people know what they should and shouldn't be posting, and there's a way to resolve any disagreements. Some of your fans may have experience with other groups; look for one of them to help "moderate" the group, and then you won't even have to be that involved. You set up the playdate, and they can play on their own!

- **Fan club.** A "fan club" sounds like a bit of an outdated notion, but it is not at all. If someone can "join the team" for free (in exchange for some contact information), and you give them some tasks, chances are you'll get some great engagement.

Story: The Doubleclique

Early in our career, the Doubleclicks started our own fan club called the "Doubleclique." The "club" doesn't do a whole lot, and they don't have a way to communicate with each other, but it sure was a fun way to get to know our fans.

We started the Doubleclique based on the idea that we should give people "cred points" based on who had heard of us first. Our band was very lucky to have our music shared around the Internet quite a bit, and a lot of our individual fans could rightfully take credit for "knowing us before we were cool," and helping us get our "big breaks."

I set up a Google Form (a free online survey service, discussed later in this chapter), and people filled out their name, when they first knew about our band, and their email (welcome to the mailing list, buddies!). Then we assigned everyone a number: 0 for mom, who obviously knew the band before anybody else did; 1, 2, and 3 for friends and people who came to our early shows; and so on, up to 300 or so. I then posted the list on a website called "The Doubleclique Wall of Honor for Membership Justice, Peace, Stability, Love, and So On."

This was time-consuming and very silly and a little weird (I don't think I'd make the choice to assign people "numbers" now), but it was really fun. We printed T-shirts, and people could pay to get their number printed on the shirt—a unique product that could boast how long they'd been supporting the band. When we opened pre-orders for an album, we offered the opportunity for people to pay a little more to get a special title (like "Super-President") and designation within the "Doubleclique."

None of this meant anything or cost us anything, but suddenly we had a fan club, which is pretty cool. I'd definitely recommend finding some sort of cheap way to reward your superfans like this!

Another example: indie band Paul and Storm had their fans email in a photo of themselves holding a sign that said "Minion," and these pictures were all posted up in a photo gallery on Flickr called the "Brigade of Minions," which had over 400 members before they stopped updating it. Eventually, Paul and Storm made a cool "Minion" T-shirt, as well.

Being Honest, Open, and Vulnerable as an Online Artist

When creating a big well of content and using social media, there is a good question to be asked: How much should an artist share with their fans? YouTube culture and vlogging has really shone a light on the amount of personal information that "creators" can share with their audiences. Personal and romantic details, money troubles, and mental health are all frequently discussed by content creators, even sometimes feeding a new kind of self-created tabloid culture. So, where should artists draw the line?

The more open an artist is with their audience in terms of their personal, mental, and life troubles, the deeper the connection with the audience becomes, for good and bad. If an artist is open about their struggles, fans may be more likely to share their own stories with an artist and with each other, which can lead to a very deep community bond. On the flip side, there are concerns about security, privacy, and creating a healthy sense of boundaries with "strangers" that artists should consider when deciding what to share online. There is no one "correct" answer here.

This is a financial concern as well. As more and more folks turn to crowdfunding, sometimes fans can't back everything they want to, and some frequent crowdfunders say that "perceived need" was a major factor in deciding which people to support. If an artist needs help paying their rent, if they're broke or in a tough spot, that will make a fan more likely to support them financially. On the other hand, if a musical act seems polished and has all the best tools and high-quality videos, fans may not necessarily believe their financial support is as "needed." This is complicated to consider as a marketing strategy, but does show that openness and vulnerability may be something to consider when deciding how to communicate with an audience.

Take Advantage of Coverage

Ghoul Gang's viral videos are getting a little bit of press coverage as they get posted around the Internet. That's awesome—but other than reposting those articles, how can the band grow from this? I'll tell you!

Whenever somebody writes about an artist—and I mean *any* time—the artist should make a note of it. Getting a lot of unsolicited coverage is awesome, and someday, they're going to want to spread the word about something and need to start from scratch. Let's get a running start!

Firstly, artists should thank the publication on social media and retweet/share the post. Don't be obnoxious to your followers by posting a million things in a day, but publications will definitely notice if an artist is helping them get more "clicks," or visits—which, as we'll discuss in chapter 10, is the big currency of online publishing.

Secondly, an artist should find the writer and send them a thank-you email. Chances are the writer's contact information can be found on their publication's website or through their professional social media or website. Email is the preferred professional method of communication; some journalists get annoyed by DMs or Facebook messages. This email should be short: "I saw you wrote about my band, I really liked the article, thanks for what you do!" Don't act like it was a favor. Journalists don't work for artists, and it is condescending to act like they do. Many of them don't like the feeling that a band is "trying to make friends," although that varies. The important part of this email is just to send something quick and positive, without asking the journalist for anything. Hopefully, the journalist will reply to a short, friendly message. Then, the gates of communication have been opened, and in the future if an artist has something to share that the journalist might want to write about, that artist can even reply to the email the reporter already sent, making that email much more likely to be something that they'll open.

Thirdly, bands should make a press spreadsheet, and add the writer, their contact information, their publication, and a link to the coverage on it.

Bonus: Artists can further this networking opportunity by becoming a fan of the writer. (Don't fake it, be genuine, but strategic.) Writers like and need positive comments, readers, and retweets or shares. If an artist can provide this in a genuine way, then the writer may have positive feelings about that band and recognize the name from their notifications. Then when the artist asks them for something once or twice a year, the writer will hopefully be more likely to open those emails.

PREPARING YOUR WEB AND SOCIAL MEDIA PRESENCE FOR A CROWDFUNDING CAMPAIGN

Before you launch a crowdfunding project, there are a couple more things you should get prepared:

- **Support other people on crowdfunding sites.** Back Kickstarters, subscribe to Patreons, and pay attention. This is great for research—see how it's done, and steal ideas! And it's also good optics. People can see if an artist has backed other people or if they're just jumping in trying to "take" where they've never "given."

- **Get ready to promote!** Facebook and Instagram ads are a great—and really, an almost necessary—resource. I recommend that artists set up their account for paid promotion of Facebook posts so that they know how to do it before the crowdfunding campaign launches.

Using Social Media

Twitter! Facebook! Instagram! Snapchat! Google+! Mastodon! There are many, many different social media platforms, and it can be overwhelming. Some of my clients don't want to use social media at all, and some are only familiar with one or two platforms.

Well, I'm here to tell you this—an independent online artist's job is to be easy to read and easy to access, and being literate in the main social media platforms is a valuable asset in getting the word out there.

Tips for Good Social Media Posts

- **Use each outlet as its own thing.** Sometimes, artists take a shortcut and post the exact same thing on every platform, or even connect all their social media accounts together to automatically cross-post. I see it, and I hate it! And if they take a shortcut in social media, they're making it harder for their audience to follow them. The same photo and hashtags you use on Instagram make a bulky and gross post on Facebook, and an unreadable string of characters on Twitter. Successful brands and bands are active users of social media and understand how each one works, meet fans where they live, and use each social media platform as an individual space.

- **Be a generous user, and don't just talk about yourself.** Tag and thank everybody who does anything for you. Tag events when you're there, promote shows when you're at events, and reply to anybody who talks about you!

The best way to know how to use a social network, or any website, is to look at other people and what they're doing and try to emulate their best practices.

Different Platforms, Different Posts

Before they start their crowdfunding campaign, I recommend that my clients start becoming active users of as many social networking platforms as they can handle. Here are some tips for newbies to the platforms. The "frequency recommendations" are what I suggest for bands in the two to three months prior to a big crowdfunding project launch.

Twitter

A micro-blogging platform for text, photos, and videos, with a 280-character limit on the length of posts.

Content: Twitter's a great place for funny observations, sharing links, news and announcements, interactions with other bands, and live updates from ongoing events. Ideal Twitter posts get a lot of "retweets" and "favorites," so a post that is easily shareable (and thus, something that can be interpreted and understood by strangers) is a good "tweet."

Format Tips: Twitter works best with horizontal photos and no more than one or two hashtags, since the platform is pretty clean. Balance your feed; don't just post the same news over and over again. Mix it up by sharing other people's posts, photos, and fun thoughts.

Twitter is also the most "urgent" platform, so it is a great place for artists to bring their fans before a crowdfunding campaign. Crowdfunding can be very exciting if fans can be updated in real time. It's fun to celebrate milestones together, and that's much easier if everyone is experiencing the content at the same time.

Recommended Post Frequency: Minimum one time per week, maximum seven or eight times per day (if you're saying cool and unique things).

Facebook

A social network heavily focused on sharing among friends and connections, with photos, videos, events, and games. Comments and sharing are what give value to posts on Facebook.

Content: Facebook is one of the best places for events, because it seems almost everyone is on there, and the built-in event system gets a lot of good visibility. Artists can also create their own pages, and when they do, the sort of content that does well are photos, videos (uploaded directly to the platform), and posts that inspire discussions among fans. Chase the comments! Facebook is also a great place to create and join groups surrounding various interests and activities.

Formatting Tips: Facebook is optimized for photos, especially square ones, with little or no text overlaid on them.

Recommended Posting Frequency: On your page, minimum two times per week, maximum one or two times per day. (More than that, and it will get buried.)

Instagram

Content: Instagram is primarily a photo-sharing platform, so photos are the name of the game here, and it's a great place to get artistic. Instagram is also a great place for casual short videos.

Formatting Tips: On Instagram, a creator can use up to thirty hashtags in their caption. Hashtags do tend to be helpful in people discovering posts, but I recommend only using the ones that are truly "in use" and relevant. Instagram is optimized for square photos.

Recommended Posting Frequency: On your feed, minimum one time per week, maximum one or two times per day.

Instagram Stories, Facebook Stories, and Snapchat Stories

When you have too much to say, try stories! Instead of posting ten Facebook updates or Instagram photos when you go to a big festival or have an exciting day, use the story function. People watch stories like videos. They take up the whole screen, and the audience's full attention. Stories are a bit like the middle point between a regular image post and a livestream or live-tweet. Instead of posting once a day, you can show your feelings throughout the day, or your progress on a project. Creators can just post and post and post and bring along their viewers with everything they do. Still don't get it? Check out

Ali Spagnola's challenges on Instagram or Snapchat for an extreme example of what one can do with stories.

Content: "Stories" are vertical videos that are super-casual and super-live. They are a great place for informal "life-casting" footage. People share events, jokes, GIFs, screenshots of inspirational quotes, photos, and even their day-to-day errand-running.

Formatting Tips: These platforms use "vertical" photo and video, optimized for phones.

Frequency: Update as much as you want! More than ten to twenty posts in a day can get annoying for some users, but others may love it.

Some Great Social Media Support Tools

Hootsuite and **TweetDeck** are both tools that allow creators to "schedule" their posts ahead of time. I frequently use these tools to schedule promotional posts on Twitter, so I don't have to wake up early to promote a show on the East Coast, or so I can make sure my business is still running while I'm on vacation.

Twitter Card Validator and **Facebook Link Debugger** are tools created by Twitter and Facebook, respectively, so that creators can preview the way that a link will show up on the platform. Frequently, an artist will post a YouTube video, blog post, or event hoping that the link will turn into a cool "thumbnail" image, but it just looks like a sad string of characters. These tools allow creators to preview what their post will look like, and even change and refresh the metadata associated with a link.

Canva is one of many free apps that allow artists to make professional-looking images without a graphic designer. Canva has templates for Instagram and Facebook, as well as different sizes of posters. There's also clip art!

Google Forms: A form on Google is just a survey or a form you can set up with questions—multiple choice, text entry, numbers—for anything you want. It's easy to use once you learn it (and there are lots of resources to learn how, on Google), and it's free! It can automatically export all the answers into a spreadsheet for easy analysis and reading. You can even embed a Google Form on your website! We've used Google Forms for these things:

- making our first mailing list
- asking our fans for suggestions for tour venues and cities
- soliciting ideas for songs we would cover
- starting a fan club
- calling for artists we could hire to work on a music video

Google Forms are easy to sort and read. If an artist wants to know which festivals their fans go to, or what their favorite song is, they can ask on Twitter or Facebook and have a long stream of comments to read. That works for simple questions, if you just want a brief overview. If you have more complicated questions, like where you should tour or fan opinions about products, you might ask for emails, and end up with a bunch of separate things to read. However, if you ask that question on a Google Form, you'll have a spreadsheet of information you can look at any time and analyze. Can you imagine anything more beautiful?

HOW TO USE YOUTUBE TO BOOST A MUSIC CAREER

What is YouTube these days? When YouTube started in 2005, it was a weird place, with so many fewer people making content. This is back in the day when it was rare for there to be free, high-quality material online, and there was much less competition for attention on the Internet. A YouTube career that starts in 2019 is much different than one that started in 2005, or even 2012. People have different expectations, competition is high, and YouTube as a company has different goals and priorities. In the early days, YouTube supported small creators, as they were pretty much the only ones using the service. Self-made YouTubers could make money on ads, playing their songs, or making their vlogs.

These days, YouTube is one of the main go-to destinations for all content, especially music videos. Whereas "YouTube musicians"—people who started their career on the service—used to be a big thing, these days, the biggest music stars on YouTube are the same people who are the biggest music stars everywhere else.

That doesn't mean it's impossible to get noticed. People are still breaking through YouTube all the time, now! It's just different than it was a few years ago. So, having realistic goals and expectations is important.

First of all, set up the channel for success. That means a great profile image, an "About" page that is informative and fun, and a header image that is colorful and consistent with the mood of your music. Make sure there are links to your social media, website, and mailing list on that "About" page, and keep those updated. An outdated YouTube page or a bad avatar is like going into a shop that sells great stuff, but all the cabinets and doors and windows and signs are outdated.

Next, become a fan of YouTube artists—not just the big ones, but the people who are starting out, like you. You'll want to emulate other successful creators, but not the ones at the very top. They already have a huge audience, so rules are a little different for them, and they have different goals.

Then, update your page frequently. As often as you can, dedicate time to promoting high-quality content. I think a YouTube page should have at least five videos on it when you launch a Kickstarter, and ideally every artist should keep their page updated with their most recent stuff. If an artist wants to build an audience as a "YouTuber," primarily, these days, they need to post twice per week or more, but that's really not necessary if they're just using YouTube as a supplement to other work like touring and posting music other places.

What You Need to Be Successful on YouTube

Here's what you need to be successful on YouTube:

- **Talent.** Obviously, you need to make good stuff. This book isn't here to teach you how to do that, but it's required.

- **Consistency.** Post new videos often! This helps your audience know when to come back and seek you out. ("Weekly Song Wednesday" was the peak of my band's YouTube career.) It also increases your placement in the mysterious YouTube algorithm. If you are in need of content, try posting videos from live shows. You can also make playlists where you collect your fans' videos of shows (or covers of your songs, if they've been made!) to make your YouTube channel a great landing page for all things related to your act.

- **Quality.** Make videos that are easy to watch because they are good quality—not just in how good the song is, but the video, lighting, and sound quality, too. It's not a bad idea to shower and put on some nice clothes, as well, as superficial as it is. It's often easier to watch a clean-looking person in a nice-looking video.

- **Grabbing.** YouTube has a lot of options of possible videos to watch, so your video needs to be enticing. The video should be interesting within the first ten seconds, unique, and relatable (not to everyone in the world, but to some people). It's worth it as well to make nice, eye-grabbing custom thumbnails for your videos. There are tutorials on the weird psychology of a thumbnail available online.

Interactive content works well on YouTube. Creators who take suggestions and communicate with their commenters through shout-outs in videos tend to grow an audience quickly. Some creators find benefits in being vulnerable; this is the Internet and people want to be involved with you. Showing a relatable journey is a great way to build an audience, too.

What Is Popular on YouTube?

Cover songs and parodies are hugely popular. People love watching something they're already familiar with. Many YouTube musicians find success in creating a mixture of cover and original songs.

Unique and even novelty content is also effective. If something can be shared with friends and laughed about, it makes an attractive thing to share. People want to look cool and funny, so if you can make a video that makes them look cool and funny by sharing it, that's great!

Collaborations—working with other creators—is an excellent way to build both creators' audiences.

Overall, success on YouTube requires both extremely hard work and extremely good luck. Whether you dive all the way in or just elect to use it as a place to host your videos, knowing a little about the platform will serve you well.

PART II

The Logistics of Crowdfunding

CHAPTER 3

Turning the Dream into a Plan!

The magic of crowdfunding just takes a few spreadsheets.

Hopefully, at this point, you have an idea of which crowdfunding platform(s) you want to use and have a plan to get an engaged online audience. Those are the paper and the pencil; in this chapter, it's time to start drawing the blueprints.

PREPARING A ONE-TIME PROJECT (KICKSTARTER AND INDIEGOGO)

Before an artist starts planning a crowdfunding project, they should have a clear idea of what they want to fund, when, and how they want to do it. Many clients come to me with the concept of a crowdfunding project and a handful of ideas like an album, a cover album, a tour, a video, a bunch of new fans—which is often just too much. An artist might do all of those, even in a year, but to effectively communicate a crowdfunding project, to focus on it and create great rewards, they'll need to hone it down a little bit. For a one-time campaign like a Kickstarter or Indiegogo project, it's ideal to narrow it down to one big effort, with one big statement of "why" for yourself as a "mission statement." The big idea (an album, tour, concert video) can be your "product," and the mission statement helps you add to that.

Here are some sample "mission statements" my band and clients have used in the past:

- "We really like making music videos for the Web, but we can't make money doing that, so we're on Kickstarter."

- "It's a dark political time, so we want to make happy music to help us get through it."

- "I want to make an album that will give me a shot at my 'big break,' so I'm fundraising to get an incredible PR team." Note: hiring an expensive PR company is a *very* common Kickstarter goal: look up Emma Hill and Julia Nunes for some examples. Sometimes, a PR company costs even more than the cost of producing and printing the album. It's worth it to explain to your audience how spending your money this way will help you, and starting at the mission statement level is a good way to frame the project for them.

Before launching into the full-on planning of a crowdfunding project, you need to make a few major decisions about what you'll be doing. I ask each of my clients to go through the following list before we make any sort of plans, because each project and each artist is unique. So, take a look at your situation now, and answer these questions. If you don't know the answers yet, that's okay. Just know that you'll want to have these nailed down before you start making your plan.

- What do you want to make?
- What is your monetary goal?
- What are your other goals for this project?
- What is your timeline?
- How many fans/followers do you have, and how do you communicate with them?

What Do You Want to Make?

Are you making an album? A tour? A book? A series of videos? Having the answer to this will help you choose a crowdfunding platform and narrow your marketing.

One-time crowdfunding campaigns (Kickstarter, Indiegogo, etc.) are easiest for projects that need a lot of investment at once and produce good rewards. Raising money for an album is simple to understand. Folks give you $20, you use their money to make a CD, they get a CD in exchange.

It's slightly more challenging to one-time crowdfund a project without a clear product or rewards. For example, it's less straightforward to raise money for something like a music video than for an album. People are used to getting video content for free, or at least cheap, so you'll have to be creative with rewards. Tours and live shows are also tricky, because the logical rewards (tickets) can be a logistically difficult thing to organize and sell far ahead of time. Plus, I think seeing a band on tour is seen more as "supporting the band" than "getting a product." That being said, these things can definitely be done, one way or another. One way to get around the trickiness, if you want to crowdfund a tour, is to crowdfund yourself a CD, then order extra CDs, shirts, and other merchandise, and fund your tour by selling that extra merch on the road. If you have a lot of ideas for projects you want to fund but would still be happy with your one major idea, you can use "stretch goals" to help expand your project if it's successful.

When deciding what you want to crowdfund, it's also a great idea to consider not only what you need money to produce—but also what you have *time* to produce. Crowdfunding itself is going to be a big job. You need to manage a huge fundraising project, market it, engage with your fans, and make sure everyone gets the rewards they ordered. So, when you decide what you're going to create, make sure to take a realistic look at your calendar. This might be more difficult than you thought.

What Is Your Monetary Goal?

A lot of clients come to me and think they know the answer to this question. "I think I can make an album for $2,000," they say. This might include studio time, printing CDs, and hiring a few musicians. But chances are, when you've first started thinking about a project, you haven't thought of everything. That's totally fine. This number will likely go up and down through the six-week-or-more process of planning your project before you launch it, but knowing what number you're starting with is ideal.

Once you're serious about this project, start a master "costs list," and add to it anytime you think of something new. Keep in mind: your outward-facing crowdfunding goal should actually be much, much higher than this! We will talk more about budgeting, and all of the aspects involved, in future chapters.

What Are Your Other Goals with This Project?

Crowdfunding doesn't just dump a bunch of money on your lap and run away. It will, ideally, engage your audience, create opportunities for creative collaboration, and set you a stage to make some cool decisions and proclamations.

Think about what your goals are with this project. Do you want your musical act/art to be perceived differently? How do you want your life and career to be different? And how might this project support that change? Does your album have a point of view? A new sound? Do you have something to say about art and music? Putting all of these thoughts together will work into a "mission statement" that will help with marketing to frame your project, both for yourself and for your audience.

This will also help you decide where to trim your budget. Do you just need an album to sell at shows? Then maybe you don't need to spend $10,000 on the coolest musicians and producers.

Are you trying to get noticed by big-name music press outlets, and level-up to get an agent and label? Maybe focus more on paying for PR and mastering than on an expensive T-shirt design, and don't overcommit yourself on custom rewards.

Do you want to get on the road? Maybe this project helps you make some awesome merchandise that will keep you rolling as you meet new fans.

What Is Your Timeline?

A crowdfunding project often takes a long time. I like to have as long as possible before launch to do the work of laying the groundwork—both with the project and with the audience. If you already have an engaged online audience and can easily access all the artists and producers you need to make your project happen, you may only need a couple weeks to plan your project. However, I recommend at least six weeks (or as long as possible) to get yourself prepared.

As for the work after the crowdfunding campaign "ends," build in a lot of leeway. Take a look at your platform. Kickstarter doesn't send out the money raised until fourteen days after the project funds, for example. Plus, manufacturing often has delays, and shipping/packing can take a long time.

Here is a sample timeline for a one-time project. It's a rough outline for an "average" Kickstarter project for an album. Every project is different, of course. Some folks already have their albums recorded or films made before they crowdfund them, and just need the final push for funds to print CDs or excitement for the launch. The goal of this timeline is just to show how many moving pieces are involved in creating a project, and how much time you need to set aside from "creating the art" to "marketing and promoting it" in order to have the money to make it happen.

A SAMPLE TIMELINE FOR KICKSTARTING AN ALBUM

January

- Decide on a project to create and release free content to fans, and start that project.
- Set goals for updating social media regularly.
- Decide on the scope of the album project and project mission statement.
- Research and select studio, engineer, producer.
- Calculate recording budget.
- Brainstorm reward ideas.
- Contact artists (T-shirt designers, album art creators, photographers), and reach out to manufacturers for price quotes for rewards.
- Create bare-bones Kickstarter page as a starting point.
- Make a list of past press coverage, and start researching potential coverage for the future.
- Research Kickstarter projects and bands that are similar, and learn from them.
- Back projects on Kickstarter and connect Facebook friends, to become part of the community.
- Create fan Facebook Group.

February

- Build up mailing list, and continue to engage fans online with free content.
- Release free song on Bandcamp, require email list sign-up.
- Make a plan for the Kickstarter video.
- Hire artists to create album art and art needed for merchandise (T-shirts, etc.).
- Get new press photos.
- Book any shows that you want to happen during the Kickstarter.
- Plan a new song and video to release the day the Kickstarter launches.
- Gather images and assets (show photos, testimonials, press links) that will be needed for the Kickstarter page and promotion into an easy-to-access folder.
- Write a great band bio and create a press kit for website.

March

- Research final costs and estimate shipping.
- Pare down budget to fit realistic goal for audience size.
- Make plans for stretch goals.
- Be sure Kickstarter account is ready to go (file tax paperwork and connect your bank account).
- Film and edit Kickstarter video.
- Film, record, edit launch day music video.
- Finish writing Kickstarter page, adding rewards.
- Get feedback on page from experts and other creators.
- Write press release.
- Reach out to press who need more lead time with launch day music video preview.
- Create social media and marketing promotion plan.
- Create Facebook event for launch day, plan launch day schedule.
- Draft mailing list email for day 1 of the campaign.

April

- Launch Kickstarter.
- Promote Kickstarter project online every day. (More on promoting the Kickstarter while it's live in chapter 8.)
- Perform concerts and livestreams.
- Post Kickstarter updates.

May

- Campaign ends!
- Record the album.
- Share behind-the-scenes photos and stories with Kickstarter backers.
- Send surveys to gather backer information.
- Order merchandise and rewards.
- Make a plan to fulfill all custom and personalized rewards.

June

- Send album for mixing and mastering.
- Share behind-the-scenes photos and stories with Kickstarter backers.
- Work on custom rewards.
- Send album for printing.
- Work on a music video or other way to premiere a song on day 1 of album launch.
- Begin work with a PR company on album release (if you're working with one).

July

- Share behind-the-scenes photos and stories with Kickstarter backers.
- Announce CD release date.
- Update press list, and send out album preview to reviewers.
- Tell backers to update their addresses on Kickstarter if they've moved.
- Personalize rewards (sign them), etc.
- Pack rewards and get ready to ship.

August

- Start a fun album release countdown on social media.
- Ship rewards to backers the week before digital release.
- Release album to backers two to five days before wide release.
- Write press release for music video and album.
- Send music video and press release to press list.
- Release album.

How Many "Fans/Followers" Do You Have, and How Do You Communicate with Them?

One of the biggest pitfalls of creators in goal-based crowdfunding platforms like Kickstarter—probably the main cause of project failure—is an artist asking for more money than they can actually earn, given the size of their audience. Crowdfunding platforms aren't just places where money comes from; they are places where creators bring in their audiences to work together. Crowdfunding is an intermediary, not a source. Therefore, crowdfunding is a tough place to fund an expensive first album or show if you don't first have an audience. If your audience is small, you may need to start modestly with your first project, and then use that money and momentum to create more cool art to attract a larger audience next time. We talked a great deal about how to find and build an audience in chapter 2, because that's absolutely essential.

Even more important than the size of your audience is your ability to communicate with them. There is a common wisdom on crowdfunding that a Kickstarter project needs to be funded 20 percent on day one to build enough momentum to succeed, and that 20 percent will come from existing fans, friends, and family. Well, that 20 percent can't happen if you don't have a Twitter, mailing list, or Facebook post that your fans will see on day one.

In the "Goal-Setting" section of chapter 4, I'll discuss how you can research other similar musical artists and their successful projects to see what a "realistic goal" is for your project, given your audience size. For now, remember that building an audience, and being able to communicate with them, is a fundamental pillar of a successful project.

INTERVIEW WITH HAYLEY ROSENBLUM (PATREON MANAGER FOR AMANDA PALMER)

Hayley Rosenblum is a champion of creativity who specializes in fan engagement, helping artists build lasting relationships and community with their fans online.

As a longtime, integral member of musician/artist Amanda Palmer's management and digital marketing team, for nearly a decade, Hayley has conceived and executed boundary-redefining digital engagement initiatives that have helped Palmer shape the way for independent artists to use the Internet to connect with their fans.

Since 2016, Rosenblum has had an essential role in managing the daily operations of Palmer's Patreon community, which has over 11,000 patrons fueling Palmer's independent art each month (which includes webcasts, music videos, songs, performance art, animations, podcasts, and documentaries).

Rosenblum served as Kickstarter's Music Outreach Lead and Campaign Strategist (2013 to 2016), working with thousands of musicians, including many of Kickstarter's biggest music campaigns, to develop digital marketing and fan activation strategies to fund their creative projects.

Amanda Palmer creates intensely personal art. Do you think that this personal honesty has a relationship with her success on crowdfunding? Does crowdfunding create a responsibility to be vulnerable and personal?

I think that there are different ways to explore crowdfunding that you can be comfortable with, if you're an artist who doesn't want to be very personal, and doesn't want to overshare what's going on in your life and creative process. That being said, Amanda's approach is to be very personal and very open. In doing so, she definitely builds trust within her community, and that trust is the underlying essence of her success. Because she trusts her community, her fans, her backers, her patrons, her supporters—because she trusts their opinion and recognizes that they trust her and what's she's doing to make art and how she's doing it, it's a two-way street and builds upon her relationship with her community.

The people giving her support aren't beneath her; they are part of the whole process in making and enjoying her art. That fuels the way that Amanda talks to her community. That fuels all the transparency that she provides, because it's a relationship that has honesty from both sides. Amanda will ask for feedback, and she'll get honest critiques and criticism and that fuels everything forward. She's authentic to her audience, and they return that honesty back to her.

How much work needs to be done before launching a successful and artistic crowdfunding campaign like yours?

I would suggest, for anyone who is new to starting a crowdfunding campaign, subscription model, membership platform, etc., that they think very deeply about what their goals are, what they're trying to accomplish, what success looks like or means to them, and be mindful that success may not mean hitting a crowdfunding goal. It may be bigger or simpler than that, and unique to what they are making.

Before launching a campaign, plan and research to learn more about your audience, understand what your fans and your community want, who is your audience, and where are you going to find them. How will you reach them? You can launch a crowdfunding campaign or subscription platform, but if you haven't thought about who you're reaching out to—who your audience is and what they want—you may confront some difficulty once the campaign is live. You may feel like you're not being successful, when in actuality, you have so much potential to achieve the goals that you have but you may not be resonating or even reaching the very people who are most interested in supporting you.

What's your favorite thing that has come out of making art with your community through crowdfunding?

The thing that drives me is that I'm a fan of music, and I love the connection that I have with art. So, for me, the big motivation is to help foster community and connection around art, whether it's with Amanda or other artists. I deeply respect how music and art bring people together. My personal favorite thing is seeing people deeply moved and connected to the work that we're doing for Amanda and the work that Amanda's doing—seeing people incorporated into the artwork, seeing them connect with other people in the community, which is really amazing.

Just as an example to illustrate, we just put up holiday cards for sale for "patrons only" through a post on Amanda's Patreon page, and someone wrote a comment on the post longing for the card and said they wished they could get it. Another patron saw the comment and replied, "Why can't you get it? Can you not afford it? What's your address? I'll buy it for you!" and they emailed me, knowing that I'm the go-to person for Amanda to help patrons out, and they asked me if I could help connect them to the person who wanted the card so that they could buy it for them.

It's this beautiful thing where, it's not just people buying music or buying art, or giving an artist money; it's people fully invested into the community that's being created around Amanda's art, and willing to go above and beyond to pass on that goodwill and positivity to each other. That, to me, is the most beautiful thing. It's a very human thing happening through a digital platform.

Does the artist and their team need to be invested in the page too, in terms of spending a lot of time updating it, to get that kind of investment from fans?

I don't know that that's inherently a requirement. I think that there are community strategies that you can implore if you're only active in spurts or active at certain points, but I think it all comes down to building the trust of your audience.

If your fans know that you trust them as a group, they will help encourage them to trust each other. It's like leading by example. If you make your community a safe space or safe place for people to be honest and interact with each other, and you feel comfortable interacting with them, that encourages them to interact with each other.

Amanda's very open to her fans and open on Patreon. She'll often ask questions and for feedback about whatever she's working on. She'll ask simple things like, "What do you think about this?" or "What color should this be?" or she'll share something vulnerable about her life and that makes people feel okay about sharing things that are vulnerable in their own lives to each other. I think there's a way to foster community even if you're only posting once a month or once every time you have a project, or if you're doing a campaign with a finite timeline (like it is on Kickstarter or Indiegogo). You can communicate in spurts. Any way you do it, if you lower the veil a little bit, other people will start to feel close to you and each other.

What do you wish people would know before they approach you for advice or help?

I think the biggest thing to recognize here is that we're all trying to figure this out at the same time. There is no definitive way to define success in this arena. It's a lot of trial and error. We don't have definitive answers, and we're all learning as we go along. What's working for Amanda may not work for someone else. What's working for your peers may not work for you.

I'll often get emails that are, "Quick question: give me some crowdfunding strategy," which always makes me laugh and think to myself, "To YOU, that's a quick question, but if I'm going to give you some advice about your crowdfunding campaign, or membership/subscription platform, I need to sit with you. I need to learn who you are, who your art is appealing to, who your fans are, and have a deep conversation about what you're working on and what your expectations are."

And I don't necessarily have time to do all of that for everybody who asks, so I do my best to guide people to where they can find some more information and help them get on to a path that will lead them to being prepared.

So, I think it's important for people to understand that there is no set way, there is no rule that says, "This is what you have to do, and it will work." Asking for advice is very important, and you should certainly talk to other creators, other artists, and their teams about what they're doing, what's working, what isn't working, what they've learned, etc. But recognize that when you say, "Give me advice," it's a large, complicated ask that may not have a simple answer.

I would add this: Sometimes, if something isn't a success, like a crowdfunding campaign on a goal-based platform like Kickstarter, if it doesn't meet its funding goal and it feels like a failure, you can still get takeaways that will help you, especially if you take all that you've learned through the whole process and decide to try again. I'd encourage artists to not to get discouraged by what they may perceive to be a failure, because it can be a really good teaching moment and help reveal ways that may even be more valuable than if they reached the funding goal the first time.

PREPARING AN ONGOING CAMPAIGN (PATREON, BANDCAMP SUBSCRIPTIONS)

An ongoing campaign has a lot of flexibility, even beyond the choice of platform, or do-it-yourself option. As mentioned in the previous chapter, Patreon gives creators the option to organize and charge "by the month" or "by the project." Even beyond that, the amount of time a creator dedicates to an ongoing campaign, like through Patreon, can vary from basically nothing to a full-time job.

Before launching a campaign of this type, there are some major questions creators should ask themselves.

- What do you want to fund?
- How much time do you want to dedicate to updating your page and sending out rewards?
- Who is your audience, and what do they like?

What Do You Want to Fund?

What are you going to use this money for? Is it to fund a particular project—like hiring actors or directors to make a music video or to buy studio time? Or is it to pay you for your time to make things? Is there a minimum amount of money you need to make it worthwhile to create this art or crowdfunding page, or are you just looking for some additional income on an artistic endeavor you want to make anyway?

Knowing your costs and monetary goals will help structure the campaign, goals, and rewards that a creator makes.

- Campaigns that update consistently—regular music videos or demos (at least monthly) that can give regular "rewards" or behind-the-scenes access.

- A "tip jar" for content that is being produced and released for free already.

- A big project that is broken into little pieces. I've seen folks find success creating a novel on Patreon because they release a chapter every month.

How Much Time Do You Want to Dedicate to Updating Your Page and Sending out Rewards?

Are you aiming to create a brand-new job for yourself, a "set it and forget it" tip jar, or a new home for your existing community?

These are important questions to ask, because ongoing crowdfunding projects have a lot of range as to what they can be and how much time they can take up. There is a correlation, of course, between the amount of work you put in to the project and how much money you'll get out of it, but it may not be quite as strong as you think. Sometimes, supporters will give the same amount of money, regardless of the rewards provided. Where you spend your time and money is up to you. Do you want to be able to dedicate a lot of time to making music, or do you want to spend your time engaging with and fulfilling rewards for your supporters? Of course, you can do both, too, but many creators find themselves overcommitting on campaigns like this and burning out.

A common pitfall with projects like this is that creators run out of time to fulfill the promises they made, either because they over-promised, or because the project doesn't provide enough income to give creators the time to fulfill those promises.

Ongoing campaigns work best when there are regular updates or signs of progress. Folks want to know that their money is going somewhere. However, any amount of update is okay—weekly, monthly, semimonthly—as long as the people supporting you know what to expect upfront.

Rewards on Patreon can range from just a "thank you" to access to behind-the-scenes blog posts, to downloads of all your music, to regular online hangouts, phone calls, concerts, mailing postcards, or merch. Basically, they can cost nothing or everything in terms of time.

Once you have a clear idea of your project, you'll be ready to head into chapter 5 to make your big choices on goals, tiers, and so on.

Who Is Your Audience, and What Do They Like?

Having a large, engaged audience on day 1 is not as essential for an ongoing project as it is for a one-time project. With no deadline, there's no "cut-off" for "failure" the way there is on a Kickstarter.

However, before launching a project, it's still beneficial for a creator to have good communication with their audience, so that they know the kind of rewards and communication their crowd would be interested in. Don't know? Ask!

FOR ANY KIND OF PROJECT

What Are Your Strengths and Weaknesses in Crowdfunding-Related Skills?

The more things you can do yourself, the more money you can keep instead of hiring other people to do it. So, think about your own skills. Do you paint? Do you tweet? Does someone in your band have skills with graphic design or video editing? Who's good at Instagram, and/or who has a sister or family member who can teach everybody how to do these things?

What will you need to work a lot on? Who can you get to help you?

The skills involved in running a crowdfunding campaign are basically the same as running a business. You'll need to make a plan and stay on schedule, keep track of your finances, and be reliable. You need to communicate effectively with both your audience and with other professionals (like reporters, podcasters, bookers, and other bands).

However, crowdfunding also creates the opportunity to buck norms and lean into strengths. You don't need to rebuild a standard label structure from scratch. You can ignore things you don't care about and make a new kind of business based on your strengths.

I'm a strong believer in the concept that if you can't do something well, do something else.

My band could never make professional-looking videos, so we leaned hard into making very cheap-looking videos that are still fun to watch. We can't put on a mind-blowing stage show, so we focus on putting on shows for cheap in weird locations. I don't have an eye for design on posters, so I invest my money in paying artists, instead of making something garish and unpleasant in Photoshop. Fortunately, my bandmate is great at recording and mixing music of our specific genre, and she also spends her time developing new skills—so we stick to our instruments and sound and as she learns more, we grow in that direction. Chances are, there are a lot of skills you already have, so let's use those!

Now is a good time to evaluate your skills, and even ask a few friends: what are you good at, and what do you need some help with? While you're running a crowdfunding campaign, you want to play to your strengths, and ask for help with your weaknesses.

The impression of competence is important when you ask for money. You need to seem like you know what you're doing, because people are giving you their hard-earned cash and want you to use it wisely.

Go through this list and indicate your ability level for each skill, and then figure out how you're going to make each item happen. Can you do it yourself now, will you be able to do it after you learn a bit more about it, or should you delegate it to someone else? (Who?) Hopefully, by the end of this book, you'll be able to add a few more checks to the left column.

Skill Chart

	Me (Now)		Delegate		Me (Learning)
	People say I'm good at it	I think I'm good at it	I know someone who has it	I need to find someone who has it	I'm reading a book about how to do it right now
Twitter					
Facebook					
Instagram					
Spreadsheets					
Budgets					
Making a to-do list					
Staying on task					
Scheduling tasks for each day					
Writing messages to my mailing list					
Asking fans to sign up for your email list					
Asking fans to follow you on social media					
Taking selfies					
Taking professional photos					
Drawing or creating professional-level album art					
Using Facebook/ Instagram ads					
Researching how to learn new skills					
Keeping track of money for taxes					
Selling yourself					
Writing blog posts					
Editing video					
Directing videos					
Making low-budget music videos					
Using YouTube to post videos					

Getting views on YouTube					
Making thumbnails for YouTube videos					
Mailing a lot of packages					
Finding artists and hiring them to help					
Sending emails to news outlets					
Appearing on podcasts					
Home recording of audio					
Performing live, keeping the beat, being engaging					
In-between song banter					
Looking professional					

FIG. 3.1. Skill Status

Asking for Help

How'd you do on that list? If you find that you may be in over your head, here are some resources to tap as you move forward:

- **Peers.** Find or create a community of artists who can share skills. I personally run and/or am a member of several "independent musician" Facebook groups specialized for people of my genre, gender, and interests where marketing folks can help budgeting folks, who can help engineering experts—all with their own set of skills.

- **Crowdfunding Platform Websites.** Kickstarter, Indiegogo, Seed&Spark, and pretty much every crowdfunding platform has created resources for artists with suggestions and how-to's on each of their platform's specific tools. You can contact the platforms directly with your questions as well.

- **Crowdfunding Consultants.** While there are a number of predatory "marketing" and "crowdfunding consulting" companies out there, there are also some legitimate experts who can help with coaching or even implementation of a crowdfunding project. Kickstarter and Indiegogo have both vetted some experts, posted on Kickstarter.com/experts and entrepreneur.indiegogo.com/directory.

- **YouTube.** It seems to be a current rule of the Internet that if there is something that you want to do, someone has made a YouTube video explaining how to do it.

CHAPTER 4

Planning a One-Time Campaign

The possibilities are endless! AAAAAHHHHH!

Once you've started to gather your plans for the project, it's time to nail down some numbers. First, we'll create a realistic goal, based on what you need and what you can make. We'll get just the perfect rewards and tiers to meet your goal and your fans' needs, and we'll combine it all together in a spreadsheet.

Your goals, your rewards, and your budget will all be developed together, so though this chapter is organized linearly, know that you'll likely get some information while researching reward tiers that will make you change your goal, and vice versa. And then when you start spreading the word about your project and it funds, the numbers will keep changing! It's important to be flexible and to stay on top of this information—and we'll help you create a spreadsheet to do just that.

GOAL-SETTING

A Kickstarter "goal" is the amount of money that you ask for on Kickstarter. If you reach that number, your project "funds," and you get the money! If not, you don't. On Indiegogo, creators can opt to earn money even if they don't reach their goal (with a higher fee), and some platforms allow creators to keep their goal private. In this chapter, we'll assume that you want to raise enough money to fit your goal.

When you set a goal, you need to keep two things in mind: the minimum amount of money that you need to make something, and the amount of money you really think you can make, given your audience.

What You Need

A lot goes into a Kickstarter campaign—more than you might think. Perhaps you're looking for $5,000 to get into a studio for one week and record your album. That's great, but your Kickstarter goal shouldn't just be $5,000; you'll also need to budget for a few additional expenses.

I recommend making a list, or spreadsheet, with the "flat costs" associated with your project, and keep it updated before and during your campaign. If your campaign gets bigger than you expected, that may mean you'll be ordering more CDs and rewards than you initially budgeted for, so don't let your costs get away from you. It's surprisingly easy to lose money on a Kickstarter campaign, and even easier when the campaign makes more money than expected.

Spend a good amount of time before your project having honest conversations with all of your contractors—producers, artists, photographers—about how much money you might owe them by the end of the project. Talk to whomever will produce your CDs or other physical merchandise as well. Having an accurate and detailed budget is vital to making sure you ask for enough money.

Rewards

When people pledge to your campaign, they'll get something in return. Whether this is shirts, CDs, buttons, stickers, or something else, you need to budget for them.

Kickstarter is a great way to make an up-front investment in merchandise, which you can later use at shows. If they can, I typically recommend that artists order twice as many CDs, T-shirts, and other merchandise than they need to fulfill the campaign, especially if they tour. This way, after your campaign ends, you can keep making money on this Kickstarter-invested project.

Shipping

Shipping is one of the trickiest elements in your crowdfunding world. The Kickstarter platform allows you to add on shipping to reward prices, which is useful. You can indicate different shipping prices for the U.S., Canada, and other countries, and I recommend that you do that. You never know, even if you've only toured in the U.S., someone's aunt in New Zealand may just stumble upon your page and feel inspired to give!

I recommend that my clients, if they are sending out more than one hundred or so packages, use a service like Endicia or Stamps.com to print postage from home. This will save you time and keep you from being "that guy" holding up the line at the post office. This also means you can estimate your shipping at home before you launch, which is essential.

Before launching, gather some items the size and weight of each of your reward packages, and enter the data into your shipping software. This software will tell you what your shipping cost needs to be for the U.S., Canada, and rest of the world. But don't stop there!

Flat costs associated with shipping include: buying envelopes, buying labels for shipping addresses and postage, printer ink, paying the monthly fee for your online postage software, and buying or renting a postage scale. This can add up. Don't forget it!

There are also companies who will handle distribution and shipping for artists. Some of these companies were founded specifically to help with crowdfunding distribution. Obviously, this involves added cost, but it might give you peace of mind and allow you to forgo the need to gain additional expertise. If you plan to hire one of these companies, get a detailed quote, and add their cost to your budget.

Currently, Kickstarter includes the costs of shipping as money that will go toward your goal, so if you make $5,000 and $500 of that is "shipping fees," that money is not going to be stuff you can spend on recording and printing CDs. This is why I use a dynamic spreadsheet that accounts for both flat and dynamic-reward costs when estimating what I need my goal to be. I'll explain this later in the chapter.

Fees

Kickstarter takes a 5 percent cut of your total money raised, and their payment processor Stripe takes an additional 3 to 5 percent cut of each pledge. Indiegogo takes 4 percent if you reach your goal, 9 percent if you don't. GoFundMe only charges credit card fees. Those fees may change, so make sure you do your research before creating your budget.

And there's more. If you use a service like BackerKit to manage your reward surveys and add-ons, they will often take a percentage of your project as well.

Taxes

I am not a tax expert and cannot officially advise you on this, but this is what I will say; get a tax expert, like a CPA. Get professional advice on how much you may end up owing in taxes and add that to your budget. If you are not interested in hiring a tax professional (though I recommend doing so; they can end up saving you money due to their knowledge of tax code), do a lot of your own research.

Kickstarter can help a creator raise more money than they've ever had before, and that does not come without a price. The money earned on a crowdfunding project may be taxable as self-employment income, and if this is the case, depending on a creator's household tax bracket, you may have to pay up to 50 percent or *more* of your gross income in taxes. This amount will change with a lot of variables, so getting an expert on board early is a wise plan. This expert may help set you up to pay estimated taxes so that you don't end up owing money all at once. I myself tend to owe around 35 percent of my income in taxes, and I've run into many situations where I wished I'd planned ahead and set aside the money beforehand. Don't be like me! Plan ahead!

A tax expert can also help you know what sort of expenses you can "write off," so talk to them, and get yourself ready, and start keeping track of everything you spend on this project. From printer ink to photography, every cost associated with your business should be tracked.

It's also a good idea to look into setting up a separate business (like an LLC) and bank account where your business money can go, if you've never done that before.

Time

Running a Kickstarter takes a lot of time, on top of writing songs, scheduling musicians, and recording an album. It's an emotionally taxing process. Don't forget to pencil in some money to pay yourself! If you need to take time off from your job, or to cut back on lessons or commissions, keep that in mind when you're planning your campaign. Budget and timeline should go hand-in-hand. Don't forget yourself!

Those Other Little Things

There are a lot of little costs involved in making an album. Don't let them sneak up on you! For example:

- Submitting your music to iTunes, Spotify, ASCAP/BMI, and distribution services like CD Baby
- Paying a lawyer to work on copyright with you, or copyrighting your album yourself
- Facebook ads
- Shipping CDs to radio stations
- Hiring a PR firm to help launch your project
- Submitting your project to *Billboard*-chart tracking services (like Indie Hitmaker)
- Paying a booking agent for a tour (if you're going on a tour)
- Hiring someone or buying equipment to make videos (if you're creating a video)

What Your Audience Will Give You

I know you have a dream for your Kickstarter campaign. You'll make the best album ever, with high-quality production, string and horn sections, music videos, a live juggler at every show, a tour van made of cheese—so you just add up those numbers and ask for that, right?

Not exactly.

This isn't the case for all types of online fundraising campaigns, but for crowdfunding projects having to deal with art and personality specifically—like many music campaigns—most of the backers are going to be people that are already familiar with the creator.

Through my years as a crowdfunding consultant, I've found I can pretty accurately predict how much money an artist will make in an ideal Kickstarter campaign, long before they launch it. It's not a scientific or guaranteed system, but there's some pretty easy eyeball math one can do to make a rough estimation of a good and realistic goal. Of course, the amount of work that someone does promoting a project, and how fun and interesting the project is, will have a big influence on the number of backers as well, but this can be a good starting point.

First, I look at campaigns run by similar artists to the client. I'll write down how many folks backed their project and how much they earned on Kickstarter. Then I'll add up average Twitter followers, Facebook likes, and YouTube subscribers. Then I look at more active indicators: Spotify listens, social media likes and comments, number of shows and the size of venues where they're playing, and other behaviors of active and current fans. I put all of those numbers into one spreadsheet and then look for patterns.

| Artist | Genre | Followers/Subscribers | | | | | Total | Avg. | Kickstarter Backers | Kickstarter $ | % of Avg. Followers Backing | Avg. Kickstarter Pledge | Recent Active Followers/Viewers | | |
		Twitter	Facebook	Instagram	YouTube	YouTube Views on a Recent Video							Instagram Likes	Facebook Reactions	Sum
Boochia Fearsano	Singer/Songwriter	3,661	782	1,354	148	80	6,025	1,205	243	$6,858	20.17%	$28	40	8	48
Becky Grapes	Scottish Folk	1,281	4,396	953	262	594	7,486	1,497	170	$7,318	11.36%	$43	100	150	250
Sandwich Zone	YouTube Punk	4,721	16,000	5,442	47,861	3,000	77,024	15,405	325	$14,888	2.11%	$46	400	65	465
LinLin Madiera	Singer/Songwriter	420	1,600	1,061	168	60	3,309	662	255	$15,152	38.52%	$59	50	30	80
The Doubleclicks	Nerd Folk	9,000	9,009	2,506	16,364	2,000	38,879	7,776	1,870	$72,406	24.05%	$39	80	200	280
Big Ted & His Medicine	Alt Rock	44,100	17,000	9,716	164	35,000	105,980	21,196	3,817	$165,104	18.01%	$43	600	700	1,300
									Projected Intake		Avg % of Followers Who Back	Avg. Pledge/Backer			
Ghoul Gang	Ghost Punk	600	1,000	2,000	400	100	4,100	820	156	$6,725	19.02%	$43	100	15	115

FIG. 4.1. Social Media Community Comparisons. This chart compares numbers of social media communities and Kickstarter earnings for a few projects at different sizes. These numbers are averaged and used to project a goal for a new client (Ghoul Gang).

Look for patterns and anomalies. For example, Sandwich Zone has a large number of YouTube followers, but they seem not to be as engaged in recent years (given the current number of YouTube views or Instagram likes). Consider whether or not this is throwing off your numbers, and how this relates to your current fan base. The more data you have, the better you can predict what your own result is likely to be, and the less they will be skewed by any single outlier.

From what I've seen, from large projects to small ones, you aren't going to get more backers than you have social media followers. You'll get just a fraction, usually between 15 and 30 percent. Potential clients approach me all the time saying "I have 3,000 followers, and I need $50,000 to make an album. If they each buy a $15 CD, it'll be fine." This is not going to happen. Probably 20 percent or less of your followers will back your project. It may be fewer if you haven't been active recently. The good news is, the average donation tends to be $30 to $50.

On Momentum

There are three main types of one-time crowdfunding campaigns in terms of funding:

- Campaigns that never meet their goal.
- Campaigns that just barely meet their goal at the end after a month of agonizing push.
- Campaigns that fund quickly and then keep funding higher and higher "stretch" goals as time goes on.

Either of the last two options are totally great, and definitely have their advantages and drawbacks. The first one is a learning experience.

I think it's better to ask for a lower, more realistic amount of money than a higher, "stretching it" kind of money, because people like to back a winner. This may be counterintuitive and frustrating, but many backers—especially casual fans or new fans of a project—will be much more excited to back a project that has already met its goal. There are some folks who would rather only back a project that super "needs" them, but for the most part, people want to make a sound investment in something that's already popular.

For this reason, I tell my clients to start small. What is the smallest amount of money you can ask for and still be happy? Maybe, for you, that means just five hours in the studio and hand-drawn album art you make yourself, for $800. That's great. Maybe it's more than that; maybe you won't be happy unless you have a full band and professional mastering. That's great too. Don't cut down your budget so much that you won't be happy with the result. Just pare down to your bare needs, and start there.

A client of mine, Josie, came to me with an initial plan to raise $12,000. She wanted strings, horns, mastering, CDs, shirts—the whole thing. But it was her first campaign, and we weren't sure how active her audience was online. Her folk music community consisted of a lot of older people and offline fans who didn't comment on or like her on social media, and her email list was relatively small. We decided to pare down her project to a basic singer-songwriter album, and set her initial goal at $8,500. We still built in a full album to that budget. If that's all she made, she'd still be happy and she'd still make something great without losing money. We launched with that new, lower goal, and Josie's project hit its funding goal in three days. We spent the rest of the month adding stretch goals for additional instruments and goals to her project.

Josie ended up raising over $15,000. I truly believe that if she had asked for $12,000 to start with, she would have struggled in the first week and ended up with less money. It's so much less "risky" to back a winning horse. How frustrating, right? That's the game!

"Stretch" Goals

Stretch goals are a frequently used concept on platforms like Indiegogo and Kickstarter. Although they aren't built into the Kickstarter system, stretch goals have become a common part of the conversation about crowdfunding. Stretch goals come into play when a project has met its initial goal, and a creator adds an additional goal if more money is raised, for more creative content, rewards, or improvements on the initial goal. Stretch goals typically come in at higher dollar-amounts, but sometimes creators use stretch goals for a landmark number of backers or different sorts of participation, like social media followers or fan-created content.

Effective stretch goals enhance the project, add to the fan experience, and allow the artist to make something they're excited about. Fun low-cost stretch goals include making a low-fi music video, covering a song your fans vote on, or adding a small prize to every physical package (like a sticker or button). Other fun stretch goals at higher levels include: the creator will get a tattoo based on the experience, or will be able to quit their day job/move to a new city!

Don't create stretch goals just because you want to get more money, or that add more work for the creator without a suitable compensation. Remember, just because the project raises $1,000 more, that doesn't mean you're going to pocket that $1,000. Here are some common stretch goals that are a trap:

- Goals that increase your workload. More money doesn't make you work faster. More money doesn't move your deadline back. You are going to think this doesn't apply to you. You are going to forget this. Try not to. This includes:

- "We will make another album!"

- "We will learn a brand-new skill and produce something using that skill!"

- "We will add something complex and personal to every order!"

- Goals involving other people: getting more people involved means *more work* for you, not less. Think about this when planning stretch goals. My band decided to add a coloring book as a stretch goal to our first project, thinking "this is something where all the work is done by our artist friends, not us." That is not true. If you're a good collaborator, that means you are a project manager, and that involves a lot of work in creating clear communication, providing feedback, paying people on time, and so on. Don't add people onto your project thinking it will reduce your work load.

- Goals that reduce the profit margin on your product more than the quantity increases it, like sending everyone a coffee mug. (Shipping coffee mugs is a lot!)

- Goals that involve your project stretching far into the future, like starting a weekly podcast or producing a musical in two years. If possible, make your project something that can be all done and tied up in six to eight months, so you can move on to the next thing. (You can always launch another campaign for the next project!) It's hard to take a break when you still have Kickstarter work to do, paid for by your eager, vigilant, generous fans.

When to announce stretch goals: I don't recommend announcing or posting stretch goals until a project is funded or nearly-funded, because it can seem a bit like hubris. I like to announce stretch goals at the same time an artist celebrates their project funding. However, if a stretch goal is a big part of your project, you may want to publicize it earlier. For example, if you want to press your album onto vinyl, go ahead and tell your fans from the get-go on your campaign page, "My initial goal is $3,000, but if we reach that, my next goal is vinyl!"

Holding on to stretch goals until a project funds can also allow a creator to reorder and reset stretch goals at appropriate amounts of money, if the project is funding more quickly than expected. For fun momentum, stretch goals should be things that can be funded in two to five days, and shouldn't reach over 200 percent of what the project has already raised. Stretch goals are a fun way to enjoy a month of continued success and celebration; just don't set yourself up for too much work!

Ghoul Gang Stretch Goals: Early in Campaign

$3,000	You're Never Alone with Your Friends: The Album
$4,000	The CD gets a lyric booklet!
$4,500	Exclusive buttons for all backers w/physical rewards!
$5,000	Online CD release party!

Ghoul Gang Stretch Goals: Later in Campaign

$3,000	You're Never Alone with Your Friends: The Album
$4,000	The CD gets a lyric booklet!
$4,500	Exclusive buttons for all backers w/physical rewards!
$5,000	Online CD release party!
$5,500	The music video for "Ghost Party"!
$6,000	The band gets extra shirts for TOUR MERCH!
$6,500	Backers vote & the band covers a song of your choice!

FIG. 4.2. Stretch Goal Images. Early and late in a Kickstarter campaign.

When budgeting for stretch goals, remember that "extra money raised" doesn't have a 1:1 relationship with "extra profit." Chances are, even if a project gets $5,000 past its $20,000 goal, there is only $2,500 or less "extra" money that can be used to pay for stretch goals, after fees and taxes. These projections can be calculated once your project starts, and I'll explain this later in the "budget" part of this chapter. It's a good idea to alternate goals between free/low-cost items and expensive, big goals, so that momentum can continue without running the project into the red.

REWARDS

What are called "rewards" on Kickstarter are called "tiers" on Patreon, "incentives" on Seed&Spark, and "perks" on Indiegogo. Different crowdfunding platforms are trying to connote different vibes with their different language, but we're going to call them "reward levels" for simplicity.

When your supporters give money to your crowdfunding project, you can give them something in return. How wonderful! For some people, just the knowledge that they are helping make art exist is the primary reason for giving. A great reward level not only gives that feeling, but also entices your supporter to give a little bit more to bring home a product that they really like. Crowdfunding supporters list "a cool reward level" as the second-biggest reason they back a project, after wanting to support an artist they already like.

So, let's build you a great set of reward tiers! Typically, a project will have five to eight reward "tiers" at different price points, each tier often including a few products. First, we'll explore what makes a good and bad product, and then organize these different rewards into packages for your fans.

What Makes a Good Reward?

Merchandise

The first kind of reward that works well for a music crowdfunding project is music. Digital albums, physical CDs, and vinyl are the most logical rewards, and sometimes, they're all an artist needs to create a great project! There's nothing wrong with keeping it simple. Check out Jonathan Coulton's Kickstarter for his album *Some Guys* as an example of a sleek campaign.

Do you still need to sell CDs? Do people even still buy them? Some people do, to be honest, and it's a great product in terms of mark-up. Backers say they like CDs for their cars and to have them signed. It's worth it to ask your audience whether they need CDs. If you don't think you're going to sell them, you can skip them, but you may be surprised at the money you're leaving on the table. That being said, some of my clients have run successful album Kickstarter projects for their albums and completely skipped the CDs.

Merchandise beyond albums adds one more layer of complication to the project, but it can be a great way to make more money. Whenever a band creates merch, they'll do better if they work hard to create an attractive product with great art and great quality. Fans want to wear or own something that will get them compliments, even from folks who don't yet know about the band on the shirt. Investing in a great artist is important. Merch is also a great way to connect with fans. If the shirt, pin, or sticker is something they like, they can wear it or see it on a regular basis, and the band becomes a bigger part of their life.

If you don't already know a great artist or designer, finding a good one can seem tricky. However, there are thousands of affordable designers and artists that you'll run into if you look in the right places. We go to a lot of comic conventions, and a walk around "artist alley" is an amazing showroom for independent artists and their styles. We've also found artists by asking musician friends, and by just researching who has done the art for merchandise we've liked in the past. That big community of creators that we mentioned in chapter 2 is a useful resource for this sort of thing. It's worth it to ask fans if they know artists, too.

Ask fans for advice and recommendations as to what kind of rewards they'd be interested in. This sort of question can build hype for your project and make for a fun social media discussion. Take this advice with a grain of salt, of course; fans may not know how expensive it is to create a particular item, and they each have their own quirky, individual taste. It may be a good idea to provide a set of options so fans can vote on their favorite, and/or to reach out to a small group of superfans to have specific questions about pricing or specific reward combinations. And if a fan wants something you don't want to make, don't make it. You're going to spend much more time in this crowdfunding fulfillment than they are!

With any reward, it's a good idea to keep in mind the profit margin as well as how difficult it will be to ship to backers. Try not to produce any items that can't be bought for 30 percent or less than what you can sell it for.

Easy products:

- Digital albums. Don't even have to ship it!
- Digital back catalog. A wonderful reward for new fans and people who may have not bought your music yet. Plus, you don't have to mail it!

- CDs. And you can have a higher level for a "signed CD!"
- Custom enamel pins. They're trendy, small, and can usually be printed for $2 or less, and sold for $10 or more.
- T-Shirts. Invest in a great design, and you could be your fan's new favorite shirt!
- Tote bags. Even better than shirts, because they fit everyone!
- Zines. A little, stapled-together book with your thoughts, drawings, etc. It's got the feeling of being personal and exclusive, but you don't need to make a brand-new thing for everyone.
- Stickers. They're so small, cheap, and fun! Find a great printer online of die-cut stickers to make something that will stick to laptops and car bumpers.
- Buttons. These are tricky because you can't charge very much for a button, but they make a great "exclusive" reward if you make one that is only available through the Kickstarter. Then your fans can wear them at a show to boast that they're a great supporter of you!

Difficult products:

- Posters. Hard to ship without getting crushed.
- Vinyl records. Also hard to ship and expensive, usually with a high minimum order, but they work great for certain audiences.
- Books and coffee mugs. They're heavy, and therefore relatively expensive to ship.

Creative Rewards

Crowdfunding provides a great opportunity to look beyond "expected" merchandise, to new and different kinds of rewards that focus on a musical act's personality and talents! I've seen Kickstarter projects where musicians painted pictures of fans' pets, called fans on their birthday, created role-playing games and dice, taught piano lessons over Skype, even done life-coaching sessions. Ideally, a fun and creative reward can fit into the theme of your project and your band, to make a really neat, cohesive experience.

The great thing about creative rewards is that they can be extremely fun without being expensive. The trade-off is that they might become time-consuming. Keep a realistic idea of how much time you'll have to create custom and creative rewards while also producing the "main" portion of the crowdfunding project. It may be smart to make a sample so you can see how long it takes to create this creative or custom item.

What Makes a Good Reward Tier Spread?

In addition to choosing some great different "products" and experiences that will be used as rewards, a creator also needs to organize those different items into a set of rewards that fans can choose from. Typically, a campaign will have three to ten reward levels (I recommend five to eight), ranging from a low amount like $5 or $10 to really high—$500, $1,000, or even $10,000. It's a good idea to provide rewards at various levels for different kinds of fans. I typically have rewards get more personal as they get more expensive.

A common pitfall in creating a set of reward tiers is making it complicated. It's easy to get carried away and to create a lot of reward tiers with a lot of pieces of merchandise in various combinations. Chances are, you don't need to do this. I ask my clients to narrow their product ideas down so that they have just eight or so reward levels, and each increasing level is a comprehensive combination of the rewards from the previous level with one easy-to-understand addition or change. See the sidebar, "Sample Reward Tiers."

SAMPLE REWARD TIERS

Here's a series of easy to understand rewards:

$10:	Digital Album
$25:	CD + Digital Album
$50:	T-Shirt + CD + Digital Album
$60:	Digital Back Catalog + Digital Album (New Fan Reward!)
$80:	Custom Drawing by the Band + T-Shirt + CD + Digital Album
$300:	Request a Cover Song + T-Shirt + CD + Digital Album
$900:	Life-Coaching Session + T-Shirt + CD + Digital Album

As for pricing—and this is the tough thing to remember—charge more than you would in a store. If a CD is $10 in a store, on a crowdfunding page it can be $15 or even more. A shirt that is normally $20 at the mall can be $40 on your page. This is a crowdfunding project. The mark-up exists to help fund the creation of the project, and most of your audience will likely understand that. There is evidence showing that people are going to spend roughly the same amount of money regardless of the available reward, so it's not necessary to pile a bunch of cool stuff into each reward level.

Pricing custom, creative, and participatory rewards is tricky, too. If an artist is offering to create original songs, paintings, or other one-off custom items, it's hard to know what to charge. Start with the minimum you'll want to charge to feel like it's "worth your time." Custom rewards take a long time. And remember, all that money is going to the project (and taxes), not necessarily into your pocket. To arrive at an exact price, I recommend performing lots, and lots, and lots of comparison research. Look at pages for other musical acts of a similar level as yours, and see not just what their reward levels are, but how many people actually backed them. Alt rock superstar Ted Leo can charge more for an original song or hangout than a band with twenty fans and one year experience in the industry. Sometimes, it can be hard to tell before you launch whether $300 for a cover song is too much, too little, or just right—and you'll never know for sure. Doing some comparison research can really help.

When creating your page, the reward tiers will be on one side of the page while your "story" about your project is in the middle. I like to keep the number of rewards down so that the "reward" column isn't longer than the "story." A simple selection of rewards will make it easier for a fan to make a quick choice, instead of getting overwhelmed, leaving, and not remembering to come back.

When looking at the reward tiers you've built, here are some questions to ask:

- Is the reward selection simple and easy to understand?
- Can you picture the fans who will back at each level?
- Does it provide a good spread for fans at different price points? Keep in mind you don't need to cater to every single fan, it's better to have a streamlined set of rewards than a bunch of rewards with just 1 to 3 backers at each of them.
- Are you avoiding giving folks "too many different things" at each level? If someone just wants a CD and T-Shirt, for example, do they have an option to get that without a hat, a button, a sticker, an umbrella, and four or five merch items they may not be interested in?

- Is there good enticement to increase a pledge? Does each increasing reward add something of a well-priced value?

- Are there rewards for fans who want to participate to get something custom and cool, and for those who just want to buy something and move on?

- Have you optimized "no shipping required" rewards? Are there more great things you could make without ever having to send a physical item?

Story: The Year of Eighty Custom Rewards

When my band launched our first Kickstarter, we did the thing most people do; we got very excited about making the dollar number go up as fast and high as possible — and it did! We reached our $18,000 goal on day one and eventually broke $80,000, becoming the biggest music Kickstarter to date in Oregon history. We offered lots of custom rewards and kept offering lots and *lots* of stretch goals that put a lot more work on our plate.

One of the custom rewards we offered was a "cover song request." For $250, a fan could request a song, and we'd cover it and make a video of us singing the song. It was a hugely popular reward—popular enough that the ten we offered were claimed on the first day, and we offered five more of them at $300. $1,500 + $2,500 = That was $4,000 right there! So much money!

And then we had to make them.

Turns out, a lot of songs people like are really complicated. Someone requested "Smooth Criminal"—and we're a twee ukulele/cello folk band.

These took *forever* to finish. In addition to twenty custom short songs, and fifty hand-drawn-colored illustrations, we'd basically signed ourselves up for six months of work on top of making an album (and fifteen music videos, and an EP, which we have yet to finish four years later).

We spent long weeks in the studio learning and performing cover songs for these videos—weeks that we couldn't spend writing new songs, or doing gigs, or making more money. It was certainly fun, and we loved that we got to play our fans' favorite songs for them. But it was a lot of work—work that didn't serve our whole fan community, just the people who ordered and liked those specific songs. I don't regret doing it, but I do regret not fully thinking through how much work it would be before we started.

It sapped our energy and took us away from finishing the stretch-goal EP and new music that I wish we could have been focusing on. For the crowdfunding projects after that first one, we made less money, offered fewer custom rewards, and had a much more reasonable workload.

BUDGET ON KICKSTARTER

Now that we've talked about goals, rewards, and reward tiers, you may be getting your head around how complicated your budget's going to be. If not—welcome to a fun time!

Budgeting a crowdfunding campaign is tricky. Chances are, you won't know until your project is over what exactly you'll need to spend all of your money on. You won't know how many T-shirts or CDs you need to order until you know how many people pre-ordered them. If you have custom-made rewards and commissions, you'll have to budget separately for those things. Shipping is a huge question mark. International shipping and domestic are incredibly different prices. You get the idea. Let's fix it.

Budget Spreadsheet

Your budget spreadsheet should have two major parts: flat costs and variable/reward costs, and then a third sheet to combine them together.

Flat costs will cost the same no matter how many people back your project. This is your studio time, mixing and mastering, submission fees, prices for PR, and photo shoots. This will also include big-ticket items that are relatively static. For example, the price to produce CDs, vinyl, or stickers will likely be part of your "flat costs," as you will probably order a round number (200, 500, 1500, whatever) and not change that based on how many people order your album. (Maybe it will jump up, but not often.) Your flat costs section can be simply a list of costs and a total. It may be a good idea to keep notes of "minimums and maximums" if things are variable in price and you can't nail them down (for example, if you aren't sure exactly how many hours you'll spend in the studio).

ITEM	COST
Studio Time to Record Album	$900
Mixing and Mastering	900
Payment for Studio Musicians	900
Music Video	600
Duplicating CDs	800
Facebook Ads	100
Digital Distribution (CD Baby or TuneCore)	60
Mailing Supplies (envelopes, labels)	80
Shirt Design and Shirt Printing Setup Fee	120
Stickers	80
TOTAL	**$4,540**

FIG. 4.3. Flat Costs

The reward costs section tracks items that change as your number of backers change: T-shirts, postage, custom-made rewards that you're hiring people to make, things like that.

CAMPAIGN DETAILS			COST				INCOME		
Reward	Pledge Level	# Backers**	Cost to Make	Cost to Ship	Cost Total Per Item	Cost Total	Income Per Unit (including shipping)	Gross Income	Net Income
			Per Unit*	Cost to Make + Cost to Ship	Total Cost x # Backers		Pledge Level + Cost to Ship	Income Per Unit x # Backers	Gross Income – Cost Total
Digital Album	$10	160	$0	$0	$0	$0	$10	$1,600	$1,600
Physical CD	25	60	0	5	5	300	30	1,800	1,500
Physical CD + Buttons	40	71	6	5	11	781	45	3,195	2,414
Digital Discography	50	24	0	0	0	0	50	1,200	1,200
Physical CD + T-Shirt	75	24	12	8	20	480	83	1,992	1,512
Premium Package	100	51	36	8	44	2,244	108	5,508	3,264
Custom Ringtone	120	1	75	15	90	90	135	135	45
Custom Song	300	1	75	15	90	90	315	315	225
House Concert	1,000	0	120	15	135	0	1,015	0	0
		392				**$3,985**		**$15,745**	**$11,760**
		Total # of Backers				Total Reward Cost		Total Gross Income	Total Profit

*Ignoring CD production here, because, since they have to be produced in quantities of 500, that is included in flat costs

**Estimated (based on other projects by other bands)

FIG. 4.4. Variables/Rewards

I list the rewards early on, and then look at projects from similar artists to estimate how many folks will back at each different reward level. The spread of backers can make a big difference for the income of your project: 90 backers ordering a digital album at $10 costs nothing and earns me $900, while 12 backers ordering a T-shirt at $75 (plus shipping) also adds $900 to the money earned but adds $200 to shipping and production costs. Depending on what rewards people select, hitting a goal of a certain amount of money can mean making *or* losing money, so playing around with possible combinations on this spreadsheet is an important step to be sure a project is asking for enough money.

Once the costs are handled, I enter those numbers into the "summary" tab of my spreadsheet, but that's not the end of it. There's still some math to do to add a safety net—money to save for taxes, and the crowdfunding platform/credit card processing fees. Often, putting all the numbers together like this, including estimated numbers of backers, will lead to a "scare" that shows that I'm not asking for enough money. That means it's time to go back to the drawing board and play with the numbers until they don't end in being broke.

INCOME	
Total Raised	**$15,937**
COSTS	
Total Flat Costs	4,540
Total Reward Costs (Projected)	4,177
Safety Buffer (20% for overages, taxes, etc.)	3,187
Kickstarter/Stripe Fees (8%)	1,275
Total Cost	**$13,179**
Final Profit (Total Raised – Total Cost)	**$2,758**

FIG. 4.5. Summary Sheet

The takeaways from this budget talk are this: everything is going to cost more than you think it will, make simple but fun reward levels, and charge enough for them.

INTERVIEW WITH MEREDITH GRAVES
(Director of Music at Kickstarter)

Meredith Graves is the director of music at Kickstarter. Prior to starting that job in 2018, she was a correspondent for MTV news. Meredith is also the front woman of the punk band Perfect Pussy and runs her own label, Honor Press.

What do you think successful creators spend the most time on, regarding a Kickstarter project?

THEIR SELF-CONFIDENCE! Their motherf*****g self-confidence, which I know you can't print. They work on themselves.

The most successful Kickstarter creators are the ones who put in the most difficult work—more difficult than raising money, more difficult than learning how to play your instrument—the difficult, nearly impossible task of actually recognizing that no matter what you've been told, in your life, it's okay to ask for help.

They work on undoing the decades of societal abuse they've experienced that have told them that music isn't a "real job," and they don't deserve s***. The creators that are most successful are the ones who commit to that work before they commit to learning how to edit their video, before they try to figure out what their newest, biggest, most special reward tier can be. They work on undoing the feeling of unworthiness that we all seem to come with factory standard, simply from being born into the world we're in. So, the most satisfying campaigns, the most successful, might not even fund, but they leave people in a better place.

Is there an optimal way to create a Kickstarter? Is there math for, say, the right number of Kickstarter updates?

No! Hell no! I tell everyone from massive, national museums to individual creators who are still six months out from signing up for the website the same thing. One of my favorite things in the world is to come up with totally new and hilarious ways to use the site. I've done this successfully with Sacred Bones Records, with Don Giovanni, and other small labels that have run campaigns for other reasons than just making money.

You can have a very low goal and fund in one day, and maybe you don't need that much money to visit your project, but you need millions and millions and millions of people who come to Kickstarter every day to see your name on the front page of the site. You just put in a couple days of work to get free PR for the thirty days that your campaign is running, and that's sick!

I've heard of people trying to run Kickstarter campaigns as part of an augmented reality game, I've seen people run their campaigns in character. So no, there are literally no rules.

I backed to completion a campaign a few weeks ago coming out of somewhere in Australia because it made me laugh until I was blue in the face. It was a speed metal band that wanted to raise two hundred dollars to hire ballerinas off of TaskRabbit for their record release show. I was like, "Take my fifty bucks, I don't give a s***, I'm the director of music, this is hilarious."

The best campaigns are the most creative ones. The most successful campaigns are the ones that are enjoyable for the creators who are running them. Kickstarter isn't the music industry, and thus, things about the music industry and what we call "the process" that are painful, we don't have to engage with them, over here.

That's why, frankly, I really don't care if people think there's a big stigma about having to ask for money. If some dudes in a band that have been around for thirty years and have got gazillions of dollars from a label don't think Kickstarter's going to make them look cool—congratulations! Enjoy the rest of your career literally everywhere else, because over here, we're having fun. We're hiring ballerinas off of TaskRabbit. It makes me super happy that I can say, with as much authority as the person in charge of music at Kickstarter has, that music at Kickstarter's a party, and this is what we do now. The most successful campaigns are ones that are a joy to run.

How important is it to have an audience before launching a Kickstarter project?

Part of the stigma around community funding and music is, because we're all sort of affected and infected by late stage capitalism, we have a tendency to believe that if we were good enough, people would just be offering us money, as if that's something that happens—ever—to anyone.

"Audience" is a natural word that we turn to when we start to talk about music and performance, but really what you need, and what people deserve, is less of an audience and more of a community. That's something that Kickstarter can both nurture and provide in some cases, and I'm really proud that I'm able to say that.

I would say that having a community for music is important for musicians in many more ways than for Kickstarter. It is important to have an audience, because it's important for us to be able to test our music on people. It's important for us to feel safe and supported and to have a community around that will give us feedback, that will support us ideologically as well as financially.

One thing—a line that I've held firm to—is that Kickstarter is nothing new, and that passing a hat around the basement at a hardcore show is the original crowdfunding. It's easy to support one another, and in independent music scenes, we've been doing it for years. I think having that audience is important for the same reason having an audience for an independent band is important, even if you're not going to do a Kickstarter, because even if nobody has money, people can definitely promote the music. They can hang flyers, they'll be happy if their band is on the same show as yours.

What are the coolest rewards you've seen for a music project on Kickstarter?

The most satisfying rewards I've seen my creators make are the ones that make maximum use of their existing talents and don't kind of play into the industry/consumerism aspect where they feel like they have to make a bunch of new stuff for their campaign. I've seen some really novel stuff. The Aquabats said they'd buy someone an island.

The rewards that I see that actually are actionable and do well are things like for a low reward tier, giving new backers access to their back catalogue. The strange thing about that is, even a five or ten dollar pledge on Kickstarter will still get an individual artist, in the end, more money than 40,000 streams on Spotify. So, low-goal access and education-based rewards are exceptional.

I have great educational creators who say, "I'm not a cool musician and I'm not putting out a record. I'm just a teacher. What do I do?" Do you realize that your ability to teach is a reward that is priceless? Like, please give people the gift of your research and charge them for it. That's great.

My personal favorite recently was a man from upstate New York who is an incredible educator and a very, very funny person who runs a project through Kickstarter called "Metal Guitar Academy." Because of the overwhelming success of his campaign, he decided to provide everyone who backed the project with an early, free PDF release of his book. It's a basic guitar education book that when you get up into the advanced stages just steers you directly into speed metal. I mean, I've played guitar since I was 11, and I'm 31, and I've learned more from the first six pages of this book than I've been able to teach myself in 25 years. It is the sickest thing I've ever worked with, in my life.

How does Kickstarter fit into the relationship between independent artists and labels?

There's not a binary between labels and independent, because every label is different. Of course, while I say these sorts of things, I cop to the fact that I am signed to a label, I have multiple record deals, I have a label that used to put out my old band's records, I work with labels constantly.

What I'm concerned with is the multinational, all-encompassing capitalist realist scam, that in order to be a musician, you have to take certain steps in a certain order.

What's going on here really is that I'm trying to reverse engineer a bunch of information about the music industry that should be very transparent, but isn't. If it remains occulted, you'll have to hire so-called professionals to do it for you. Musicians think they need PR, they think they need management, they think they need a booking agent. And they might need some, all, or none of these things, but it's not a checklist that you have to go off in order to be successful.

So, if you've stalled around the "finding a label" step, and you think that Kickstarter is just your step to getting that— no. Kickstarter is the step that makes it so you actually don't need that because you can then pick and choose what it is you want to do, and you'll have the money and the resources and the connections to reach out and force those pawns on your own without an intermediary.

There may be artists who are already on labels whose labels haven't optioned their most recent output, but they still like it, and they still want to put it out. So, they're going to release it independently, knowing that their label may still distribute it; they just need to cover the recording and pressing. Maybe you do want to be on a label, but maybe you want to get your record done first so that when the label approaches you to put it out, you own the rights to your music, and that's not a question.

Every label offers something different, and decrypting what it is labels do is what's going to help musicians everywhere. More specifically, my creators set reasonable goals for how much things cost. It alleviates peoples' worry. No one wants to look under the hood if they don't know how to fix their own car. I'm really trying to make the resources and information as valuable as the money, if not more so. So, while they're funding the project they actually want to make, people can alleviate some of their stresses simultaneously by taking back the means of production.

What resources should artists check out with regard to Kickstarter advice?

I realize the one biggest thing that people don't realize about Kickstarter is that we're people. This company is roughly a hundred or so people who work in the same office, and we're looking into each other's eyes all day while we're actually building the software out for the site.

If you need to reach out about a music project, I'm the most accurate weather forecaster in the world. Hundred percent chance that it's gonna rain down on my inbox, because I run that category.

If you're having technical difficulties and you email our support system, you're not just filling out a form that gets filed into nowhere; it's going to the person who's sitting next to me in the kitchen. And if it's specific to music, look around at the projects on the front page of Kickstarter.com/music, because I'm the person who puts all of them there. It's just me, one person, one girl with a bunch of face piercings and a dog that follows me around the office. I'm a human, and I'm actually here to help. And I'm not hard to get in touch with.

CHAPTER 5

Ongoing Campaigns

This project starts and just keeps going,
so build a plan you won't regret!

The logistical details for an ongoing campaign, like a Bandcamp subscription system or Patreon campaign (or one you make yourself), can range in complexity from much easier than a one-time campaign to much more difficult. In all likelihood, an ongoing campaign requires less shipping (if any at all) and possibly no production of physical items. However, if you get real wild with it, it's possible that this will be much more complicated. Because people can back your campaign at any time and there is new content happening all the time, you'll have to spend a little time every month on it, and it doesn't have a clear "end date" eventually, like an album cycle does.

Ideally, the logistics of an ongoing campaign—reward tiers, goals, and most parts of the schedule—should serve the purpose of supporting the art being made. This is easy to lose track of. I'd warn you, don't pull yourself too far away from that goal. Don't sign yourself up for so much work writing thank-you sonnets or calling fans on the phone that you don't actually have time left to make music!

Supporters say that they tend to back Patreon projects for one of two reasons: to support an artist that seems to need support, and to get access to behind-the-scenes or exclusive content or communities. These backers are often more interested in you making art than you sending them presents, so focus on that as you make your decisions. (But, as always, follow your bliss!)

If you completed the questions in chapter 3, you are well on your way to making a project that fits right into the sweet spot of rewarding your patrons while giving you enough time to take care of yourself.

CREATING TIERS

A "tier" on Patreon (and the different ways different sites call "Levels") is a set reward level that a supporter can select. Typically, this will be what they are charged every month (or "per creation," as I will explain in the "goals" section below) to support you.

You can have as many levels as you want. Patreon recommends five or fewer. A minimum level of $1, $2, or $5 per month is standard for most fans. Keep in mind that there are a lot of monthly subscription services these days, so you should try to be "worth it." Even if your "rewards" aren't something people care about, you should be creating enough content to be worth a $5/month minimum donation. That would mean some sort of post weekly or at least twice per month. If you're making something less frequently, a "per creation" pledge may make more sense than monthly—but all of this is dependent on your project and what you want to do with it.

For example, if you're planning to release a song every week on a regular schedule, a "monthly" donation makes sense. You're releasing a lot of content and the frequency will not change, so folks know what to expect to get for their money. Reward levels can be at $1/month to see behind the scenes, $5/month to download all the new songs as mp3s, $10/month to get chord sheets, and $20/month to get an annual postcard from the creator.

For another example, if you're just using Patron to fund an occasional music video, a "per creation" pledge may be better. This way, your patrons are only charged when they know they're getting something in return, whether it's twice a month or twice a year. Reward levels could be at $1/creation to get each song as an mp3, $3/creation to get chord sheets, and $30/creation to get a personal shout-out in the video credits.

Most Patreon projects have a few rewards: something at the low level, a few at the $5 or $10 per month, and then some high ones at $20, $50, even $100. Keep in mind this is a regular donation, so that is a really substantial pledge. It's important to offer rewards that you can follow through on rewarding.

"Rewards" are less important on Patreon than they are on somewhere like Kickstarter. People back a Kickstarter at a $20 one-time payment, and they are going to be waiting for that CD to come. If someone gives $2/month to your Patreon for music videos, they may watch the music video and never download the MP3 of the song that you sent them. That's okay! Some fans do like rewards, so it's not a bad idea to provide them. But when creating a page, take care to promote not just the rewards, but also the idea of your band supporting and participating in your art. Patreon acts a lot more like "patronage," the idea of supporting an artist's life and making it possible, so keep that in mind when creating the page.

The "rewards" people do seem to be interested in on Patreon are exclusive offerings. These could be behind-the-scenes videos, early recordings of songs (there's even an option on Patreon to release stuff early to your backers, and publicly later), or even just exclusive content that the public will never see. If you are banking on people being excited about this "private" content, you'll definitely want to have some public examples of those cool things, both on the page, and on the rest of your social media as you promote the project. Artist Kate Leth does a great job of advertising her Patreon-exclusive content through previews on her Twitter and Instagram pages.

The "rewards" that are harder to make and promote, and take a lot of time, are those where you have to make stuff specifically for your patrons, not just for the "art" of it. I've seen a lot of these from folks who get overwhelmed: I'll write you a sonnet, I'll do a 1-on-1 coaching session with you, I'll have a monthly Q&A Google hangout with top-level patrons, I'll mail you a postcard, I'll send you a T-shirt. These are really fun! These rewards are also a little more time-consuming than mailing out rewards on Kickstarter, because though there may be less of them, they aren't all happening at once. You have to be ready at any moment to start a new custom reward, even if you're on vacation or in the middle of recording an album. I caution creators away from offering this type of reward if they can avoid it, unless it's something that they would really enjoy making. Likely, your fans are more interested in helping you make art than they are in getting their own unique things, and they'd rather you spend time on your art.

These custom rewards can be extremely successful, however! If you want to go this direction, schedule your time, how you're going to fulfill these rewards, and how you will keep track of what you've done. Patreon will allow you to ask for mailing addresses and any other information you might need up-front, so be sure to ask for all that information. It can be quite hard to track down backers to fill out a survey after the fact.

It is up to you how much time you spend on individual rewards, versus how much time you spend making art exclusive for Patrons, versus how much time you spend on art for everybody. Remember, creating custom rewards will take more time than you may think, and you have to do this stuff all year round.

There is a middle ground between "no reward" and "complicated reward," and that is offering rewards like immediate access to a back catalog of music, a piece of art in PDF form (like a coloring page), or other digital reward. These downloads can even be posted on the "thank you" confirmation page that every patron will visit immediately after backing a project, so you won't even have to send out an email with the rewards.

GOALS AND PROGRESS

Creators are not required to set a specific goal when they create a project on Patreon, and the option isn't even available on other services (like Bandcamp). The option for goals on Patreon is available, though, and can be a great way to build momentum or to make a page flexible. For example, if you want to offer a monthly live show, but only if you have enough money to afford doing so, that could be a "milestone goal" that the campaign can reach and unlock. Ideally, these milestone goals will be things the creator wants to make— creations that can be made quickly, and that benefit everyone.

Good goals:

- We'll start an ongoing series (of videos, blogs, online shows).
- We'll do a big one-time event (online show, experimental new type of content).
- We'll poll the patrons of this page and make a cover song of your choice!
- We'll buy new video/sound equipment for higher-quality video.

Goals can also be added and changed after the Patreon campaign has launched.

Patreon offers an option to make the amount that the campaign is earning public, or invisible to anyone but the creator. The main reason creators I know keep the amount invisible is because a dollar amount that seems like a lot may discourage fans from pledging because they don't think there's a strong "need," but the need is truly still there. Publicizing the dollar amount can also seem tacky. But this is all up to the creator.

BUDGETING

When making plans for an ongoing subscription service, especially if you have specific plans for how to use the money, it's important to keep an eye on budget. The number you see on the page won't necessarily be what you're taking home. Pledges will bounce, as people forget to update their credit card information, folks may cancel or change their pledge, Patreon takes fees, and if you're backing other artists on Patreon, that money may come out of your income. Patreon charges backers on the first of the month, but backers usually get paid around the sixth or seventh. On other services (like Bandcamp, for example), backers can elect to be charged only annually for their subscription, so that money that's for a "year-long" project only comes once; don't run out! Other budget concerns include paying for shipping and shipping materials, and paying yourself. If you launch a project hoping it will let you cut back your hours at work, and it doesn't... well, what happens then? Keep all of this in mind when deciding what you will promise with your page.

CHAPTER 6

Creating a Crowdfunding Page

*Because everyone loves summarizing
themselves in one webpage!*

A crowdfunding landing page has a lot of weight to carry. We will get into the specifics of layout for different platforms later in this chapter. But overall, whether this is on Kickstarter, Indiegogo, Patreon, or anywhere else, this page has to serve several audiences:

- people who just want to support you
- people who want to get their money's worth
- people who don't know anything about crowdfunding
- superfans who already have everything you've already sold
- casual fans
- people who don't know you but are buying a gift for their friend who is a fan of yours
- people who have never heard of you, or your music, before
- broke people
- rich people

It's a lot. To make a page that works for all of these people, these are the basic principles for success:

Keep it short and easy to skim. It's the Internet, and nobody has a lot of time to read anything. Also, nobody wants to give money to something that they feel they haven't done all the research on. So I try to make each Kickstarter/Patreon/etc. page something that can be easily absorbed in two to five minutes. Minimize your use of long paragraphs or complicated graphics, and keep it simple.

Answer every question. Reread your page a few times from every perspective. What if someone is *brand new* to your art? Do you answer the main questions they might have? (For example: Does this person seem to know what they are doing? How long have they been making music? What do their songs sound like? When will I get my CD?)

What if this is a longtime listener, do you answer their questions? (Why is this project important right now? How is this different from what I already have?)

What about someone who is precious with their money? (Why is this worth paying for now, instead of later? What is the quality of the items I am purchasing?)

How about someone who wants to feel good about their high-level donation? (What am I making possible that would not otherwise be possible?)

This is a good place to think about why people want to give to a crowdfunding project. Some like the social capital and the feeling of having made a difference, and supporting something that would otherwise not have been created. Some want to support and get attention from a band they like, and the satisfaction that they'll have in the future that they were a part of that band's journey. Some want a cool physical thing!

That's just fans; but what about someone who's never heard of you? What would make you buy a CD from a band you've never heard of? A friend's recommendation? An awesome pitch? A cool preview track? You'll need to appeal to all of this while you make your page.

Keep your focus. Crowdfunding for musicians is "relationship-based" fundraising, instead of "product-based" fundraising. There are technologies, coolers, board games, and other products online that use crowdfunding to launch, and those have a different set of rules than music does.

Think about the difference in your mindset between going to a store to buy a new desk chair and going to a merchandise table after a concert to buy a T-shirt.

When you're buying a chair, you tend to care less about the person who made it than the quality of the chair. You want a chair that's the right color, size, quality, and price point.

On the other hand, a band T-shirt would be of very little good if the customer doesn't know about the band—or if the band isn't on it. It could be the perfect size, shape, quality, price point—but if it's not got a band logo of your fave act on it, who cares? The after-show merchandise rush captures the energy of art-induced excitement. A band T-shirt is a social way to demonstrate one's interest in a particular kind of art. And music is the same: a CD isn't just a product. It contains emotions and feelings that show something about someone's opinions and tastes and personality.

Your crowdfunding page should do the same thing. *You aren't primarily selling a product, so don't focus on that.* You're creating an opportunity for someone to involve themselves in a piece of art, to show their personality and point of view by adding a physical manifestation of your art into their life. In a beautiful way, that's an emotional connection. In the cold way, it's also why you can mark up your prices. So make a page that involves your audience in that idea.

MAKING A ONE-TIME PROJECT PAGE

The rest of this chapter will discuss how to create your "landing page"—this is, the page on your crowdfunding platform, whichever platform it is. I'll start with a basic Kickstarter-type page and then add some modifications for subscription-based services.

On each type of page, there are a few common areas.

The "Basics"

The top of your landing page will have a title, subtitle, monetary goal, and header image. Keep this simple and descriptive without being redundant. A good image is often text-less, and it is often worthwhile to get a professional photograph or piece of artwork to demonstrate the seriousness of your project.

The Story

This is the longest part of your page and the most important for communication with your audience. This will be a collection of words, images, videos, and audio samples of your work. You need to summarize your whole existence and plan in one place. I have a pretty simple starting point that I think creates a page that flows nicely and can be skimmed for people who don't need every section. Break your page into these sections:

1. Who am I?
2. What am I making?
3. Why I need your help
4. What you can get
5. Where the money goes
6. Thank you!

I like to create a strong, visual set of horizontal headers (using photos, illustrations, or just cool big fonts) with titles for each section to improve skimmability. Your return fans don't need to read "who you are," but brand-new people will want to know who you are before they are asked for money.

Who Am I?

This is a super important place to start! This is what everyone needs to know before they can give you money, and also, can be skipped by people who already know the answer.

Tell your reader about your experiences and your credits. This is the place to sell folks on why they should support you, and why you will succeed. Include quotes from reviewers, links to previous albums, and a nice image of you performing. A live performance photo demonstrates that you are a "real musical act" who has actually booked and performed gigs.

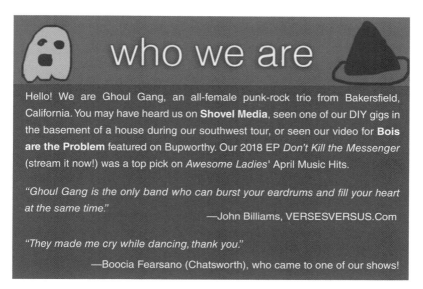

Hello! We are Ghoul Gang, an all-female punk-rock trio from Bakersfield, California. You may have heard us on **Shovel Media**, seen one of our DIY gigs in the basement of a house during our southwest tour, or seen our video for **Bois are the Problem** featured on Bupworthy. Our 2018 EP *Don't Kill the Messenger* (stream it now!) was a top pick on *Awesome Ladies'* April Music Hits.

"Ghoul Gang is the only band who can burst your eardrums and fill your heart at the same time."
—John Billiams, VERSESVERSUS.Com

"They made me cry while dancing, thank you."
—Boocia Fearsano (Chatsworth), who came to one of our shows!

FIG. 6.1. Who We Are

What Am I Making?

This is where the party gets started. I read a great piece of advice before launching my first Kickstarter campaign, that your project needs to answer these questions: Why *this* project, and why now?

The answers can be so many things. "I've been making music for fifteen years, and I've finally gotten the team I need to record an album." "This is a concept album about my trip this year interviewing dolphins in the coral reefs of Australia." "This is a series of videos about the current political climate." "I just liberated myself from my label and want to make music for me and my fans." Whatever that answer is, you should boil it down to a "mission statement," and use that to format this section, and the overall marketing for your campaign. "I'm making an album because it's time to make an album" is a good reason, but it's not a compelling story, and it won't help you make a page. It'll bore you and anyone who is reading. So come up with something that will resonate more!

This section of your page should explain everything about your project, in a basic overview. Give enough information that it is clear that you have done your planning and thought out the project completely, but don't give so much information that the page becomes hard to read. Perhaps you have hundred-word bios for each musician you'll work with, or for an artist and producer you'll hire, but you can save those for project updates later, or just link to them off-site. Give your fans enough to be excited about, without wearing down their patience.

This section works best as a narrative, leading right from the "Who You Are" section. If "Who You Are" answers the "Hi, what do you do?" question at a cocktail party, then this one answers "What are you working on?"

Explain your project, and use definite terms, as if the project is going to happen. Instead of, "We might be able to do this if the project funds," "This is what we hope to do," or "We want to make this, or possibly this," use definite language. "We will create this album, with your help!" "We are going to make a music video!" "We're creating a four-part immersive experience!" You "are creating," you don't "want to create." We've found that people want to be part of a success, and your definite language will reassure them that their money will be well spent.

To that same note, include samples! Include a track list if you have it. Provide any information that can prove that you know what you're doing and that the project is well along the way to completion.

If your project reaches the "stretch goals" stage, you can also add information about stretch goals in this section. In fact, it's a good idea to update the page during the project to reflect answers to questions as well as news, upcoming events, and goals. A Kickstarter page (and some others) can't be changed after the project ends, so if you have any final information, make sure you make those final updates before the last moments of the project!

Three years ago, Ghoul Gang got lost in a desert without a GPS or cell reception, and we missed our show. We slept in our van for the night, until finally someone drove down that long road and told us how to get back to Phoenix.

While we were stranded there, we thought hard about our band and our mission. Even though we were lost, we had each other, and we were never afraid. And that's what we want our music to be. And that's the theme of our new album: *You're Never Alone with Your Friends*.

This will be our first full-length album, and we're so excited to tackle our most ambitious project yet. We've written twelve songs, and we are working with producer Jerry Swift of Big Award Studios in Portland, Oregon (who worked with Slater-Binney!) to lay down the tracks.

Listen to a sample track here:

This is an album of ultimate pump-up jams for the Neopets generation, and we cannot wait for you to hear it!

FIG. 6.2. What We're Making

Why Do I/We Need Your Help

This is the section where you get to make your supporters feel special! One big mistake I see on crowdfunding pages comes with the balance between confidence and deference.

Too weak:

I want to make this, if you want it, I will! If not, that's okay.

Too strong:

This is your chance to get in on a once-in-a-lifetime musical opportunity!

Just right:

I'm real excited about this project, and it will be possible with your help!

Treat your backers with respect. They have given you money, for which they likely worked very hard. Crowdfunding is a form of magic, and it all comes from the somewhat unintuitive and selfless generosity of your backers. Please, please, please thank them. Don't guilt them, and don't talk down to them.

This is also a great place to give a brief explanation of crowdfunding and the platform you are using, in case Uncle Joe stops by and has never heard of Kickstarter.

You don't need to give exact dollar amounts in this section. Write with the confidence of someone who has done the math of what you need, but don't show your work. Things are going to change, and the more information you give, the more weird comments you'll get from people who think they know your business better than you. (All that being said, please do your math before you launch your project!)

why we need you

We are here on Kickstarter to ask for your help. This album will be awesome, but not without your pledges, which we only get if we reach our goal! We need your help to pay our collaborators and our studio rent, to produce CDs, shirts, merchandise, and promotional items for the album, to get the necessary software, instruments, and plug-ins, to master and mix the music, to submit the music to iTunes, Amazon, Spotify and other music stores through a distributor, and to generally "create something from nothing."

Ghoul Gang is an indie, crowdfunded operation. With no external label, agent, or manager, we depend completely on our audience to help us make our art. The advantage of that—and this is huge—is that there is nothing between us. Our music goes straight from our hearts to your ears. We love it. It means so much to us to be able to make just the thing we want and just the thing you want, too.

We thank you for supporting art and artists, and for making the world more beautiful!

FIG. 6.3. Why We Need You

What You Can Get

This is a very important part of your page! Not as important as the art you're making, but still—very important.

Most crowdfunding platforms have a separate section where people can select rewards, and that will be where you can describe each different level, the cost, and what comes with each "reward package." On the main "story" part of your page is where you'll show the rewards, post images, and give longer descriptions that might get overwhelming in that little "shop" sidebar.

I suggest putting an image and description of each item, in order of low to high cost of the reward level it comes in. Again, keep the text minimal.

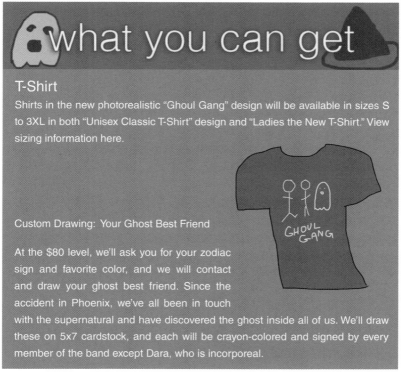

FIG. 6.4. What You Can Get

Where the Money Goes

I find it helpful to include a description or a graph of the various places that money will be spent from a project. This is a good way to illustrate to backers that the money they see being raised isn't going right into a creator's pocket; it's being spent on creating a cool piece of art. This chart can also be a good demonstration to the audience that you've done the work of calculating costs and will be able to fulfill your promises with the funds given. I typically create this chart using data from my budget spreadsheet, combining similar items to make an easy-to-understand chart.

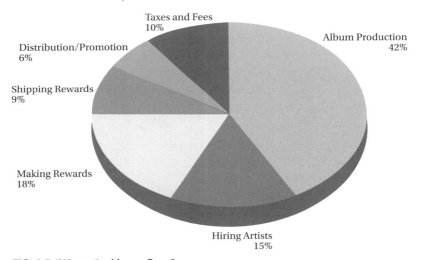

FIG. 6.5. "Where the Money Goes"

Thank You

This is where you say thank you! There are people who helped you along your way, who came to your first concert, who helped you edit your Kickstarter video, who took photos of you for free when you were still playing at an open mic. Use a few sentences to thank those people. First, because you wouldn't be here without them and they deserve your thanks. Second, because being a gracious person who remembers the people who helped them is an admirable quality, and that's the kind of person that strangers trust with money.

As you can tell in this chapter, I truly believe that Kickstarter is a platform based on goodwill, and you need to bring that to the table hard and often.

THE REWARDS/TIERS SECTION

We've talked about actually pricing and creating the rewards for your project elsewhere, but here let's talk about how to clearly communicate about them.

On the sidebar part of the page where rewards are selected, it's important to be clear and extremely easy to skim. There should be enough information that someone can select a reward without reading the rest of the page, but not so much information that there is too much to read. Kickstarter offers the option to use bullet-point item selection to make a clear delineation of each item available on your project. If you use that, avoid being redundant. Make sure the spelling, grammar, and capitalization are above reproach. Reward levels cannot be changed once they've been selected during the project.

Pledge $10 or more

Digital Album

You'll be the first to get our new album, "You're Never Alone with Your Friends!"

INCLUDES:

- **Digital Album Download**

ESTIMATED DELIVERY   SHIPS TO
Sep. 2022   Anywhere in the world

0 backers

Pledge $25 or more

Physical CD

You'll get a signed copy of our new CD, with album art by famed Aura photograper Sra M. Hews!

INCLUDES:

- **Signed CD**
- **Digital Album Download**

ESTIMATED DELIVERY   SHIPS TO
Sep. 2022   Anywhere in the world

0 backers

Pledge $50 or more

T-Shirt

You'll get a soft, hand-screen-printed T-shirt designed by Dara and made in Phoenix. Sizes small to 3XL available.

INCLUDES:

- **T-Shirt**
- **Digital Album Download**
- **Signed CD**

ESTIMATED DELIVERY   SHIPS TO
Sep. 2022   Anywhere in the world

0 backers

Pledge $80 or more

Ghost Best Friend Illustration

You'll get a custom, hand-made drawing of your ghost best friend, drawn and signed by the band.

INCLUDES:

- **Ghost Best Friend Drawing**
- **T-Shirt**
- **Digital Album Download**
- **Signed CD**

ESTIMATED DELIVERY   SHIPS TO
Sep. 2022   Anywhere in the world

0 backers

FIG. 6.6. Pledge Levels

Risks and Challenges

Many platforms now require that you fill out a "risks and challenges" section of your page. This is because there have been many, many projects that fail to follow through on their promises. Since pretty much anybody can launch a crowdfunding page, some people do so without proper forethought and they get caught off guard.

So, fill out this section, and be honest. Do *not* write, "We have everything figured out and nothing will go wrong." The only person who believes nothing will go wrong is a person who doesn't have any idea how much work they have to do. Something will probably go wrong. That's normal. A wise businessperson already knows their risks.

Your goal with this section is to demonstrate that you know what might go wrong, and to show some potential problems that you've already headed off with work. It's a bit like the "what's your greatest weakness" question in a job interview. Share the problem, and also share how you've solved it.

FOR EXAMPLE:

Manufacturing delays, illness, and other unexpected problems could come up in this process and delay the project. However, we have built some "safety time" into our schedule to hopefully make up for those problems. We have worked with a professional to create accurate budgets for merchandise, services, and shipping, so we feel good about our ability to fulfill this project on time and on budget. We've also already written all the songs, so writer's block cannot stop us!

THE VIDEO

Most platforms allow for a space to pitch a video where you can explain your project. A pitch video is a great way to demonstrate that you are serious about the project—that you're willing to invest time in making it high quality. However, a pitch video probably won't make a huge difference in how much money you raise. As long as you make a video with decent quality sound and visuals, and a semi-professional level of editing, you will meet the requirement of creating a professional pitch video. Putting personality into a video is a great idea, but don't distract yourself by spending all your time on the video to the detriment of other parts of your project. Creating a marketing plan, building your audience, writing songs, creating an easy-to-digest crowdfund landing page are all more important than a hilarious and expensive Kickstarter video.

Laser's Formula for a Quick and Easy Kickstarter Video

I suggest that you take the first few topics on your crowdfunding page (Who Am I, What Am I Making, Why Do I Need Your Help, What Can You Get?) and condense them to create a short script for a two to three-minute video. Write the script down; it will be shorter than if you try to "wing it." The video should follow the same guidelines as your page: keep it short, make it accessible for both new viewers and hardcore fans, and be gracious. Focus more on personality than product. Say thank you.

Memorize the script, and read it into a camera (even your phone) in a quiet and well-lit room. Put music underneath it, ideally an instrumental track of a song from the album. If you have video editing capabilities, overlay some images or video of your act performing live and maybe a picture of your album art. Be more thankful than clever. And please keep in mind that it feels like about 50 percent of Kickstarter videos start with "Oh, I didn't see you there." You can do that if you want, but understand that it is overdone.

Documentary Video for Beginners

Bring your band (or yourself) into a well-lit room with a clean/tidy background, whether that is your kitchen, studio, or just your couch. Use a microphone if you can, in a quiet space (not outside!), to capture your audio without hums from fans or the room.

If you don't have any video equipment, that's fine. Record the video on somebody's phone (set it down so it's not shaky), and then put another phone right next to the people who are talking to record the audio. Voice Memos on iPhone can be your recording software.

Make sure the main light in the room is on the faces of your subjects, not behind you, and clear out any distractions from the frame. Move the camera so people take up most of the picture. If you have a hard time memorizing a long script, read it one line at a time and look down at the script in between lines, and then use "jump cuts" to edit the video together. People won't notice, or if they will, they'll notice way less than they would if you were rambling or looking down at a script.

It is easy to edit between lines and hard to edit in the middle of a sentence. So, take long pauses to learn your line and read the script, then look up at the camera, pause, and say the whole line at once. If you mess up, start again at the beginning of the line. If multiple people are on screen (if you're all sitting next to each other to read this), please remember that you are on screen and everybody should look at the camera or each other.

SAMPLE SCRIPT:

Hi, we're Ghoul Gang, and we write songs about things like love, ghosts, witches, and depression.

We're a punk-rock trio from Bakersfield, California.

You may know us from our viral hit "Bois are the Problem" or from our Southwest tour, opening for the Vampire Vamps.

We want to make a new album this year called *You're Never Alone with Your Friends*, featuring songs we wrote when we were stranded in the desert with no water, shade, or beds, for almost twenty hours. It was a dark experience, but we came out of it knowing a lot about ourselves and each other.

To turn our songs into the songs of our dreams, it's going to take help from pros and lots of time on our part. And that's where YOU come in.

We've got some rewards for those of you who can back this project, like signed CDs, T-shirts, and custom ghost illustrations.

But even if you can only donate a little, you'll be contributing to our ability to make more and greater things, and we appreciate it!

We are extremely thankful that you let us make music for you, and we want to do it forever. FOREVER.

Thank you so much!

Length of Campaign/Ending Date

A Kickstarter or Indiegogo campaign runs for a limited length of time, and you'll get paid at the end of it. The classic length for these campaigns is thirty days.

Typically, a Kickstarter campaign gets the most buzz and the most funding in its first four days and its last four days. You might get a momentum boost in the middle, but usually you don't. So, a campaign doesn't need to be any longer than thirty days, and in fact, longer campaigns are actually in more danger of losing momentum or burning out your audience on constant promotion.

I recommend setting an ending date for your campaign that is twenty to thirty days from the launch date. Include the first of the month in the middle of your campaign somewhere, since that's a popular payday and some people need to schedule around that to make purchases. Fun note: inevitably, every time I run a campaign, someone will post "I'll back this after payday!" It's always a little frustrating to me, because Kickstarter doesn't actually charge cards until the last day of the campaign, so you could back it now as long as you get paid before the campaign ends.... but I digress.

End your campaign at a time of day that you, and your fans, will be watching. Perhaps, you'll do a countdown event (see next chapter!) and thus you'll want it to end right as that livestream or concert is happening. Simply put, it's fun, but not necessary, to have the end of your campaign be a climactic moment you can share with your audience, so schedule the end time of your campaign accordingly.

MAKING AN ONGOING CAMPAIGN PAGE

Note: Patreon is a relatively new and constantly changing platform, and other platforms are regularly being developed and introduced. Current features and guidelines may be different than what I describe here, but these principles should still apply. For recent specifics, use the resources on the platform's page to update yourself on best practices.

Making a Patreon page:

A Patreon page should demonstrate professionalism and show why people should trust you with their money, introduce your band to potential brand-new fans, explain why you're asking for money, and show people what they'll get for it.

The Patreon page has a few parts:

Basics

Include the name of creator and what the creator is making. If the Patreon is for a specific thing, put it there: music videos, demos, podcast episodes, etc. If you're going to be making a variety of things, that's great too. Amanda Palmer's page just has "ART" in that area, but she does take care to explain what exactly that means later in the page.

Body

The main text of your page is where you'll introduce yourself, set out your goals, and convince visitors to pledge their funds toward you. Keep this page pretty short. The decision about whether or not to back a Patreon is a pretty short one.

Who Am I

This is the easy part, but vital! Describe who you are, just in case someone who's never heard of you finds their way to the page. Link to a great video or playlist of your music where people can check out the tracks that you're really proud of, and drop a couple credits that are particularly impressive, if you have them.

This is more than just the bio you send out to shows, though. Introduce the musical artist's personality here. You aren't just a product; if you were, people could buy it once and forget about it. You're asking for investment, so invest in the page as well!

Why I Am on Patreon and How It Works

Tell your potential patrons your small and big goals. Maybe you want to make videos because you want to be a star! Patreon is a great place to get personal, because fans are supporting on a regular basis. Really, you are becoming part of one another's lives.

What I Will Be Making Here

Explain what Patrons can expect. What will be exclusive to them, and what will they be supporting that's available to everyone? How often will the page be updated? What sort of communication can they expect from the artist?

Reward Tiers for an Ongoing Campaign

Just like for a one-time campaign, reward tiers should be laid out in an easy-to-read, quick-to-skim method. It's common practice on Patreon to upload a cute photo for each level and give it a neat name. On the Doubleclicks page, for example, backers can be a "kitten," a "velociraptor," or a "super robot." Be clear with your descriptions, and if you have a list of items at each tier, put the new addition on top where it can easily be seen.

Thank-You Page

When Patreon first launched, people put a lot of work into making cute and funny thank-you videos. I think those are great. They're a fun exclusive thing for fans to buzz about, and an excellent way to build goodwill among people who have pledged to support you!

The thank-you page is also the perfect place to put links to any one-time digital rewards that your fans can download or access, like a back catalog or exclusive videos.

PART III

Spreading the Word

CHAPTER 7

Making a Marketing Plan

This is the most important part, aside from all the other parts.

Having a really top-notch project idea, a large audience, and a kick-ass crowdfund landing page are all well and good, but if nobody hears about them, it really doesn't matter, does it? Promotion of a crowdfunding campaign is absolutely vital. A campaign should have a marketing plan in place weeks before launch. There is a lot of preparation needed to get the word out and to get the momentum needed.

While your project is running, you need to be its advocate and its agent. You're what's connecting it to the world. It's your job—not the job of your friends, family, or fans—to get that project funded. And you have to do that by spreading the word.

For an ongoing campaign like on Patreon, this means periodic pushes over time. This works especially well if you're putting out new things every month, and we'll talk about that later in this chapter—because you need to do more than just make your project, you need to promote it too.

For a Kickstarter, or other one-time campaign, you've got a ticking clock and a deadline—and it's even shorter than you think. Many of these crowdfunding campaigns have their success determined in the first three days—or even the first three hours. So making a really good marketing and promotion plan before you launch is essential.

Plan to stay on top of your campaign, especially those first few days. I just finished working with a client who launched her project, and took the second day "off" because she was so tired from the lead-up to the project. The project completely lost its momentum and never got it back.

This chapter is going to be about spreading the word to your existing audience. In chapter 10, we'll talk about spreading the word to new fans via press placements, "viral videos," and those other top-down PR resources. Those are awesome. But for crowdfunding, the name's right there, you're depending on your crowd, and it's your job to get them into your campaign. They're much more important than any press you can get.

Here are the main principles for promoting your crowdfunding project:

- Make it easy to learn about—and impossible not to learn about— your project, for all your fans on every platform.
- Make a schedule and stick to it, especially for the first few days, where momentum is the most important.
- Be positive!
- Put a lot of work into promoting your project. Don't take shortcuts. You can do it!

KNOW WHERE YOUR AUDIENCE IS

This section is going to give you advice on sharing your project on social media, in real life, with your email list and all kinds of places. All that is great, but if your fans aren't already in those places, that's pretty useless. So please, if you haven't yet, read about building an engaged online audience in chapter 2. You can't have your only interaction with your fans online be asking for money. Why would somebody follow that band?

BE ONE CLICK AWAY

When I was a reporter working for newspapers in Portland, Oregon, I looked at a lot of bad websites and press releases. It was my job to do research and discover information, and to shine lights on little-known people and projects. That's when I learned that many, many people are *terrible* at communication. I'd try to cover an event, but the time, or location, or even *date* weren't available on the website. Sometimes, it was impossible to find an email address or a phone number. And sometimes—not infrequently—I would give up on writing about something because it was hard to research, and I'd just jump onto the next article.

I was being paid to do all of that, and I still gave up. Your fans aren't being paid to follow you. In fact, they are paying *you*! So it should be your number one priority to make backing your project an easy thing to do. It should be no work at all. Imagine that your fans are lazy, busy, or both. If someone is sitting on their couch and suddenly remembers that your band has a Patreon, they should be able to type a couple words into their phone—on Twitter, Instagram, Google, or wherever they use the Internet—and back the project in three minutes or less. Making that possible is going to require some work on your end. A lot of work. More work than you think. But hey, you get to make music, so, that's the point, isn't it?

This is a basic principle that will apply to a lot of the concepts behind promoting your band on the Internet: People are busy and/or lazy, so make your content as easy to access as possible. This means, sometimes, making it free. Have your music streaming on YouTube and Spotify. Post your videos on Facebook. Stream your live shows. This means more fans for your music. Maybe you feel weird "giving away your music for free," but it's the Internet. The way I see it is this: If someone really wants to get your music for free, they probably can. They could pirate it, they could steal it. Again, it's the Internet.

Crowdfunding provides a direct way for your fans to realize that they can make art possible with their money. Buying an album at Babbage's or even on iTunes rarely provides that same direct feeling of support. So while your fans give you money—in somewhere between a donation and an investment—make sure you're giving them information and access in exchange. It's good for everyone!

We talked about "being one click away" in chapter 2 when we were building your crowd. In the context of a crowdfunding page, this becomes literal. A link to your crowdfunding project should be directly available anytime someone thinks about it. It should be your Instagram link and at the top of your website. Anytime you mention the campaign on Twitter or Facebook, your link should be right there.

Additionally, it's your job to make people remember that your campaign is going on. Inevitably, every time my band runs a Kickstarter, I'll get messages a few day later from folks saying, "I missed the project! Nooo! How did I not know this was happening?" You can't avoid all of those; some people just aren't "tuned in." But remember that your fans aren't sitting around thinking about you, constantly refreshing your website. You need to provide new and interesting updates about your project constantly, or people aren't going to hear about it.

I realize all of this sounds like I want you to stand in your fans' faces and yell "KICKSTARTER" for thirty days straight (or "PATREON" for three days every month). That's not quite it. The duration of a crowdfunding campaign isn't just about holding out a hand and asking for money—and in fact, please don't do that.

What I mean by being "one click away" is just that your information needs to be at the very forefront of everyone's mind. I give my clients a checklist (coming next chapter!) to go through on the morning of their project launch, to make sure their project is right at the head of every one of their bands' social media, website, and other landing pages.

MAKE A SCHEDULE FOR PROMOTION

When people say running a crowdfunding page is a full-time job, marketing is most of what they mean, so I recommend making a marketing timeline before the project launches, to cut down on panic during the project.

During the project, you'll want to share about it on social media and to your fans in many ways. But you don't just want to share about the existence of the project. You'll want to switch it up and pull in your fans with behind-the-scenes information, debuts of tracks or demos, photos, album art, and other relevant bits of information. You'll also want to be present and responsive to milestones and questions as the project goes on.

Momentum is vital for crowdfunding projects. That first day couldn't be more important or indicative of your success.

Launch on a Tuesday, Wednesday, or Thursday—so that people are at their computers, and there are enough weekdays left to keep that momentum moving. Launch when you have a few days to keep an eye on your project. Maybe even schedule a launch event to get your audience excited, if you have a lot of local fans who like to go to live events.

Plan a bunch of awesome stuff to talk about in your first week (we'll give you some ideas in this chapter). But don't use it all! Hold back some stories, news, songs, or images for the low weeks in the middle of your project. Momentum can slow to a complete halt in the middle of a project, so make sure you still provide your fans with something to be excited about.

And then the end of your project—this can be a bang or a whimper, and that's up to you. So plan something great for your last week, maybe a livestreamed concert, maybe a new music video, a Q&A.... Imagine what would be truly exciting, and also make sure you have enough energy and photos to keep posting about your project without being boring or redundant.

Promoting the same thing for thirty days (or longer!) can be extremely tedious, but making a plan beforehand, setting aside time, and doing some of the big work ahead of the campaign can really help keep you and your audience interested.

USE DATA TO OPTIMIZE YOUR PROMOTION

Every audience is different. Some bands have fans on Twitter, some are only on YouTube, and some just pick up a flyer at a show. How will you know which of these methods are best for you, and which are working? How can you choose where to focus your limited energy? Let's get you some data!

A creator can maximize the impact of social media posts using analytics. Kickstarter, for example, has a great built-in system on the project dashboard that not only tells you where someone came from to visit your page, but how many people visited and how much they pledged to the project. Through this method, you can see if your most generous fans are on Facebook, if they just read your mailing list, or if they came from somewhere else altogether.

Kickstarter also allows creators to create "custom referral links" to help with tracking. Kickstarter will generate a URL that you can use for a specific purpose, and every pledge that comes through that specific URL will be tracked. We use these for our mailing list and to track effectiveness of specific social media posts or ads. It is nerdy and very useful data.

Referrer	Type	# of Pledges	% of Pledged	Pledged
Mailing list	Custom	28	41.24%	$1,008
Search	Kickstarter	4	15.38%	$376
Facebook first post	Custom	11	11.05%	$270
Twitter first post	Custom	7	9.00%	$220
Mailing list image	Custom	7	8.92%	$218
Kickstarter other	Kickstarter	8	6.79%	$166
Facebook group	Custom	4	3.52%	$86
Direct traffic, no referrer information	External	2	1.55%	$38
Discovery activity sample	Kickstarter	2	1.55%	$38
Facebook	External	1	.98%	$24

FIG. 7.1. Referral Data for a Kickstarter Project with Custom Tags

Most services also allow creators to connect Google Analytics accounts, so if that's something an artist is accustomed to, they can maximize their data that way.

Another option for tracking is to create custom redirect links, using bit.ly or another URL service that provides data on how many users are clicking a link. I generally don't recommend using those redirect short-links too much because the lack of transparency can scare some backers away (are you sending them to your Indiegogo page, or to some scary spam?), but they can be helpful for analytics when used in emails and other places.

MAKE IT A "THING"

Whether or not you're crowdfunding a single big project, like an album or video, it's a great marketing technique to give this "crowdfunding thing" a name. A few names my band has used: #Doubleclickstarter, #PresidentSnakes, #DCloveproblems (from a Doubleclicks album called *Love Problems*). A name adds an air of "officialness" to the project, and also gives you a shortcut for discussing it with your fans. You can also create a hashtag from this name—make sure it's unique—and this can be a hashtag you use during the whole process, from the crowdfunding campaign, to being in the studio, to the release and tour. Then, fans can use it when posting their reactions.

FIG. 7.2. Collage of Tweets Using #clicksloveproblems Hashtag. Our latest release had its own hashtag, and clicking on it brings up a great story from the recording to release and tour from this album.

CROWDFUNDING FOR THE NON-FAMOUS, WITH KEVIN COLE

This next topic was written with Kevin Cole, and it originally was published on thedoubleclicks.com. Kevin is not a musician. He's a video game developer (founder of supertry.itch.io), and one of the smartest users of Kickstarter that I know. He managed to launch a successful Kickstarter for his first video game, and has worked full-time as a video game developer based on his crowdfunding success. It helps that he's a hard-working, friendly person, for sure—but I asked him for additional crowdfunding advice for people who, like him, don't start with a built-in audience.

If you are not famous, have no fan base, and have no body of work with which to establish your credibility, you can still have a successful crowdfunding adventure. You're just playing on Hard mode. But if you have no friends, you're playing on Impossible.

Involve your friends at every step of the crowdfunding process, especially friends who aren't afraid to tell you when a thing you have made is dumb. These are the best friends. Friends can also give you that essential "first week push" of funding that gets you noticed by nice media people. If you have friends who are credible, they will (often at their own risk) add their credibility to yours.

I could go on and on about how having a diverse and supportive friend network is crucial to everything in life, but I think you get it. But just in case you don't, over 20 percent of my project was funded just by friends I met in college. Friends. Have them.

Use Kickstarter. Indiegogo is great for little (<$500) projects or larger projects that don't fit within Kickstarter's strict guidelines. It's the strictness of Kickstarter that scares most first-time crowdfunders away, but it's the strictness of Kickstarter that adds credibility to your project. If you are unknown you are fighting the credibility fight.

Crowdfunding, like every system ever constructed, is prone to abuse. Kickstarter doesn't get it right all the time, but they're constantly and loudly fighting against abuse.

Make peace with the fact you won't get rich. Sorry. Downer.

For real though, do this for good reasons. Crowdfund because you have a great idea for a thing and you want that thing to be in the world and the only thing standing between you and that thing is money.

There's no strategy for becoming an overnight Kickstarter billionaire sensation. You can, however, be an earnest creator with an idea that can make the world a little bit better. That's just slightly more possible.

Money is a thing. Let's talk about it.

Get your goal as low as you can get it before starting. How much do you need to eat? What if you ate only ramen? How's your relationship with your parents? Make any change you can possibly make to your lifestyle to get your goal lower.

The lower your goal, the more likely you are to succeed.

Sometimes, this means you have to kick someone off the project. This is sad. If it's that or no project, you have to make the choice.

Contact media folk but not through Twitter. People tend to hate or ignore that for whatever reason. Send nice, clean personalized emails to bloggers and journalists and other people who do what you do. Most will not respond, but the ones that do will be enthusiastic. Local writers are often receptive.

Finally, **make your backers feel involved.** Some backers are genuinely interested in your project, some are backing you for the status (for real), and some just think you seem like a cool person. All of these people want to be involved with you and your project. You are a cool kid living a crowdfunded lifestyle; let people hang with you. Make your backers feel welcome and special. This is double true after you succeed.

To review: Friends equals good, shipping equals bad, do it for love, you're gonna be poor, but so is everyone. Good luck!

CHAPTER 8

Promoting a One-Time Campaign

Promoting Your Project Without Exhausting Everyone You Love

Crowdfunding is all about creating and sharing your art with your fans. In this section, I'll share some ideas on how you can promote a crowdfunding campaign that gives your fans content and fun and doesn't just beg them for cash.

So as long as you're including that Kickstarter link (*Be one click away!*) in your posts, you can have a lot of fun with promoting your project. I recommend that my clients spend the months before their campaign brainstorming and creating fun things they can share—videos, songs, covers, photos, GIFs, and games.

A good promotional crowdfunding post (on social media) hits these qualities. At least the first two are necessary.

1. **Positive!** No matter how slowly a project funds, you need to be positive. I tell my clients: on day one, you are happy and surprised how well the project is going. Literally no matter what happens, that is your attitude. There may be a point in your project where you're counting down, behind your goal, and a little scared. It's okay to tell your fans that you need them, but still keep it positive.

2. **Clear and accessible for a new fan.** It's important to keep your posts concise, but it's even more important that people can understand them. For example: "Only $500 to catfish!" is not quite as good as "Our next goal on the Kickstarter for our new album is to add Catfish Jones as a guest guitarist, and we're just $500 away! [link to Kickstarter]" That way, Catfish Jones and all their fans can retweet you, new fans can see it—and they can understand what's happening.

3. **Entertaining.** Ideally, your project isn't just a piece of information about the fact that you're raising money. It should give an impression, a feeling, or even better, a new experience or information for an existing fan who already knew about the existence of your crowdfunding campaign.

4. **Visual.** Social media is full of promotion these days—ads, jokes, political battles. A visual that can give a viewer a quick impression of what you're talking about can make a huge difference. Before starting their projects, I encourage my clients to make themselves a big folder of images: from photo shoots, from live shows, and even just casual selfies, both from music events and from their day-to-day lives. These photos will be useful to post and to have as backdrops for little call-to-action images on social media. I recommend having a variety of images, because seeing the same picture over and over again for a month can be a bit boring.

5. **Urgent.** Momentum and excitement has a big influence on how people back crowdfunding projects, so keeping that excitement up with urgent and time-sensitive messages is a fun way to get people involved. For example, a creator can count down to big milestones (Will you be my 30th backer? Can you help me get over the $3,000 mark?) and offer special experiences (If we get 200 backers today, I'll post a new video!). Making a fundraising project into an "event" outside of the money aspect is a great way to keep the momentum going.

6. **Interactive.** *Be accessible to get people involved.* The most successful project creators *live* inside their pages. They see what people are talking about, they share, they make tons of new content based on their fans' suggestions, and every post is new and different. If an acquaintance of mine asks for help promoting their page, I'm going to see if they're doing a good job promoting it on their own. If they're not, I'm unlikely to help them. This is because they are asking for work from me and my audience that they are unwilling to do themselves. This also simply doesn't seem professional or like they have a good plan. On the other hand, if they're doing the best they can and still just need a little boost, I'll be happy to step in! Your fans want to help you, but this is your project, so be present, be obviously paying attention, be visibly working.

MORNING OF LAUNCH CHECKLIST

The day that a project launches, a creator hopes for momentum and excitement. There's a lot to do to change your life over from "a normal musical act" to "crowdfunding mode." Here's a standard list of things to do the morning a project launches:

☐ 1. Double-check that all of the project still makes sense (especially goal and time frame), that it's ending at a good time, and that shipping costs are accounted for. Do a final proofreading.

☐ 2. Upload your "launch day" video to YouTube/Vimeo, and get it ready to make "public."

☐ 3. Embed "launch day" video into your campaign page.

☐ 4. Launch your project!

☐ 5. Put a link to your Kickstarter in the description of your launch day video.

☐ 6. Make the launch day video public.

☐ 7. Put your Kickstarter link in an email message, and send it out to your email list.

☐ 8. Post your Kickstarter link on your artist and personal Facebook pages.

☐ 9. Post your Kickstarter in your fans' Facebook groups.

☐ 10. Post an ad in Facebook and Instagram, with a square image, little text, a short/great caption, and a link to the Kickstarter.

☐ 11. Change Instagram and Twitter bio links to direct to your Kickstarter link. (No Bitly here!)

☐ 12. Tweet about the project, and pin that tweet to your profile!

☐ 13. Write a blog post/update on your website with a link to the Kickstarter.

☐ 14. Post on Instagram about project.

☐ 15. Thank your first backers personally on Twitter/Facebook if possible.

☐ 16. Add link directly to Kickstarter on the top of your website.

☐ 17. Change your Facebook header image to a campaign-related photo with a link in the caption.

☐ 18. Send DMs/emails to your influencer friends asking them to share link to the Kickstarter.

☐ 19. Send emails/texts to family and friends asking them to check out the Kickstarter.

☐ 20. Send follow-up email to press list with a link to the "launch day single" and Kickstarter.

☐ 21. Keep track of the project all day. Like and reply to all comments.

☐ 22. Post a Kickstarter Update by the end of the day thanking people for a great launch!

GOOD WAYS TO PROMOTE YOUR PROJECT

Now that you know what makes a good promotional post, it's time to make a marketing plan. Here are some examples of content you can plan, create, and share during your month of promotion to keep things exciting. There's lot to do that isn't just posting the link over and over again.

That being said, sometimes you're going to just have to make a post that says "My Kickstarter is $4 from its goal! Can you be the backer who brings it over the top?"—and that's okay. It's boring, but most people won't mind—of course, some grumpy-boots might complain that you're asking for money too often. But here's the thing about that grumpy person: If they're going to complain that you're posting too much, they weren't going to back you in the first place. We're working on goodwill here, and if someone is grumpy, you can't change that.

Just like at a show, if you have two fans in an audience and the rest are the confused regulars or angry drunks who want to watch the game, you're going to have a better experience if you play for the fans. They're the ones who want a good show, so give it to them! So, promote this for the people who love you. It's not time to hard sell your personality to haters. It's time to deepen your relationship with your fans.

Music Videos

Music videos are the Internet's dream. We've found through the years that folks are much more likely to listen to a single track of music if there's a video attached, regardless of what the video is. In fact, I've found that the lower budget videos actually get more views, because they have an intimacy factor that helps connect with a Web audience even better. After all, you're a grassroots operation, and you need their help, so you don't need to be flashy to ask for it! Take some footage with your cell phone in a field. Perform a song live in your living room. You can edit a video together using iMovie on a cell phone these days. The barrier to entry is lower than ever.

Ideally, I like to release a new, flashy single (something with a good story) on the first day of a project. That way, you can share that video—the gift of free art—immediately before asking your audience for money. You can even put a short "ask" segment at the end of that video. Record yourself or the band saying, "You can help us make the rest of this album on Kickstarter now!" And throw it on the end of the video, with a link overlaid on the screen. Video editing is definitely a skill, but it's likely you have a friend, a couple hours, and a good example to copy from that can help you make this possible.

Demos

If you can't make a video, or even if you can, you should consider releasing demos to your crowdfunding supporters. Whether these are rough outlines on a Patreon page or basically finished tracks for the future album you're kickstarting, demos are a great way for your fans to know you're letting them in on the project. Many fans won't listen to them, because people are busy, but even the fact that they know you have tracks that you've released will reassure and excite them. Ideally, you could release a demo per week of a thirty-day project, or every month on an ongoing project. This way, when you share your crowdfunding link on socials, you can link directly to the song (using updates, discussed later in this chapter) and talk about the song instead of money. Plus, there are many ways to share a song: a link, lyrics superimposed on a photo, a short 15-second clip of the chorus on Instagram, a little doodle inspired by the song. All of these are great posts that remind people to back your project while still providing new and entertaining information.

Livestream Events

Livestream events are a way to share a live video feed from where you are, over the Internet to your fans. You can livestream on Instagram, Kickstarter, Twitter, Facebook, Patreon, YouTube, Concert Window, even Snapchat. It's best to go wherever your audience is already, so that they understand it, and also so the platform promotes the existence of the event. There are some platforms that allow viewers to tip or buy tickets for the show. These are excellent for some purposes, but if you're doing a show to promote a crowdfunding project, consider making it a free event so more people come, and you can send people to your crowdfunding page during the show.

Most of these platforms have a "chat room" where fans can interact while you stream, sending questions, requests, or comments that you can read during the project. If you think you're likely to have a lot of viewers, it may be good to designate someone (not a member of your group who will be performing) as a "chat moderator" to erase harmful comments, answer frequently asked questions, and post relevant links to topics being discussed. Fans with good taste and a good knowledge of the streaming platform make great moderators, as do spouses and friends who are willing to learn. Make sure you give these people "moderation privileges" before the stream begins. A Google search should be able to tell you what you need to know for each platform.

Livestream events can be in a few different formats. The simplest is just setting up a phone or computer at a concert and stream the show you were already going to do. This way, fans across the world can experience the show even if you don't play in their city.

Another simple option is to open up a livestream platform at your home and do a question-and-answer session, or just talk about the project and the status of your creative endeavors. You can bring your camera (usually on your phone!) around to show off the studio, venue, or practice space where you're hanging out. It doesn't have to be a lot of work, but it's still "content!"

The third option, and the one I prefer, is a hybrid of the previous two. Set up a concert where the Internet is your audience. This can also be at your home. You don't need a "studio audience," though you can have one, if you want. All you need is a computer and a setlist. During the show, in between songs, you can check in with the campaigns and the chat room.

Livestream events provide several promotion opportunities that can help fill your schedule of social media updates during your campaign.

A week before, you can create a Facebook event for the project. Tell your mailing list. Make some cute graphics and post them on Twitter and Instagram. You can even set up a poll or just ask your fans wherever they are to submit song requests from your back catalog. It's common wisdom that a Facebook post with more comments will show up more often in your fans' timelines, so those feedback-requested posts like song dedications/requests are social media gold. Plus, your fans will want to tune in to see if their request is played.

During your livestream event, the one-click-away rule is especially in effect. Imagine yourself in your fans' shoes, and imagine that they are lazy. Is there a super-simple link they can click to access the crowdfunding page? On YouTube or Facebook, putting a link right in the description of the video is vital. Other platforms (like Instagram) don't make it easy to post links, so make a shortcut. You can use a URL shortener like Bitly or TinyURL, or add a redirect from your website (something like ghoulgangmusic.com/kickstarter) so that it's easy for you to say and for your fans to remember.

A plug for your crowdfunding project is a good example of using your "positive" rule—fans may be more engaged by the excitement of your success. If they know you'll be checking the fundraiser throughout the event, they may support the project just to see your reaction. Kickstarter and Twitch have built-in notifications so you can see who has given you money while you stream—but even if you're on a different platform, it may provide excitement to check in on the numbers. That way, instead of saying "Please back the Kickstarter," you can say "Thank you Jared for backing us on Kickstarter!" Cool fans will want to make you happy and get those thanks as well.

Livestreams are great always (my band does them monthly), but they provide an especially fun way to conclude a limited-length crowdfunding project. Consider counting down the last hour of your project with a livestream. That way, you can get in some last-minute donations, and when you promote the show, folks will have a stronger awareness that your project is going to end!

Selfies and Pet Photos

A good update can be as simple as a photo of your face. If you're a musical act who does a lot of interaction this way—videos, livestreams, or photos—and if those photos get a lot of likes (keep track of what your fans like — it's fun!)—post a few photos of yourself during the project! Maybe while you're working, playing your guitar, or petting your dog. Photos of people are interesting and humans like them, and you can find a subtle or not-so-subtle way to tie this photo back into your crowdfunding page.

For example, here are some photo captions you might include:

- "Writing Kickstarter postcards today to my amazing backers! Don't know what I'd do without you."
- "Smiling because my Kickstarter is 40 percent funded and it's only been three days! Jump on board!"
- "Mittens the cat is my best friend, and I just told her how excited I am about the new album we can make thanks to your support on Kickstarter. I'm not sure she understood."
- "Band meeting at Denny's. Thanks to Kickstarter, we're going to have an incredible year! It's not too late to join in the fun!"

Live Show Videos and Tour Images

Musical acts often vastly underutilize social media on tour. I get it, we're very busy and very, very tired on the road. However, at least during your crowdfunding campaign, try to take some photos on the road. If you can, have someone film a song or two of your set, and post it on your crowdfunding page. There are lots of ways to make free content out of a tour stop. As I said, you're already working hard, so you might as well optimize the moment.

My band takes a selfie with our audience at the end of every show and posts it online. Our fans know this is going to happen, so this gives them a motivation to come to the show. And if someone didn't know this was going to happen, now they have a reason to follow us on social media: to see a picture of themselves! Even in this world where we can take photos of ourselves whenever we want, it's still extremely fun to see a picture of yourself on the Internet, especially when someone on a stage took it!

WHAT MAKES A GOOD CROWDFUNDING CAMPAIGN UPDATE?

Most crowdfunding platforms have an "update" platform that basically functions as a blog for the project. Updates are a prime opportunity to involve your supporters in the project, providing behind-the-scenes materials and bonus stories that were too long to put on the main page. I recommend that my clients post updates frequently: daily for the first and last three to five days of a project, and one or two times a week during the weeks between. I recommend making a list of the updates you'll be writing before you launch (and the project takes over your life), so that you have time to gather all the photos and videos, and even pre-write the posts ahead of time.

Posting updates on the page is also an essential way to show that a creator is serious about their campaign. If a crowdfunding page has been live for one or two weeks and there is only one update on the page, even if the artist has been keeping up with social media, it looks like they don't care. And if they don't care about the project while it's live, how can I trust them to follow through afterwards? In addition to the content listed above, here are some ideas for Kickstarter updates:

- Stories behind individual songs on the album.

- Links to other crowdfunding projects going on now that you find exciting.

- Bios of people involved in the album; band members, the producer, the engineer, the studio musicians, and artists.

- Album art reveals! Track list reveals!

- Polls and conversations with backers.

- Roundups of press coverage or even social media posts about the project.

- A feature about a merch item or custom reward that you're excited about.

- Information about the current funding status and stretch goals. When you hit a stretch goal, update immediately!

Remember, when posting updates on a page, the primary audience is going to be people who have already backed the project. Thus, this isn't necessarily the place to beg folks to back the project. It's more the area where you make people happy that they did.

Updates also serve as links to share on social media during the project. If you release a new demo or video during the project, you can embed that in a Kickstarter update and post the link to the Kickstarter update on Facebook or Twitter. Now, if someone wants to experience that new content, they'll head to your crowdfunding page, and while they're there, why not back it, too?

When posting an update, creators should include the current status of the project. What percent of it is funded, and how many days are left? Kickstarter updates go to fans' email inboxes, and they won't have that information at their fingertips right at that moment.

WHEN SHOULD YOU POST ABOUT YOUR PROJECT?

Telling you to post "constantly" isn't helpful without a schedule. If you have a mind for social media and know how your audience works, that's awesome. If not, here are some basic ideas for how often and how you should post about your project.

Creators should, at minimum, share their projects on social media daily for the first and last four or five days, and then every Tuesday/Thursday morning in the weeks between. Ideally, you can post a variety of new pieces of content each day instead of the same link over and over again.

Use the Kickstarter update for each day (ideas above) to decide what to post about, and link to the update when you have news (like a track list reveal). Give a good reason to follow the link.

Use images/art (and a variety of them!) when posting about the project. Don't just post the link over and over. Attach an image to your post, and then include the link in the text of your post.

Twitter

In the past, I would recommend that you schedule Twitter posts using an app like TweetDeck, to post at varying times between 8 and 10 a.m. each morning and sometimes at night. However, in these modern times, you never know when there is going to be a big terrible piece of news that will make your tweet look out of place, so if you can, I would recommend this strategy: Set an alarm or a reminder for a particular time each day, write these posts ahead of time (save as a draft, even), and send them out. Morning (early workday) or evening (after work Internet time) are the best times for tweets to get traction. You can also check out data on your particular set of followers using Twitter Insights to find out when the best time to post to your fans is. When creating a post for Twitter, I focus on retweetability and the post making sense out of context, and also making it something that makes sense if it's being skimmed.

Facebook

You can schedule these on your page to post at various times, and I recommend doing that if you don't want to be constantly tuned in to Facebook at the right moments. I usually just post something different to go live at 9 a.m. each day. If something timely happens (a new update, stretch goal reached), you can update additionally, but you want to be sure that something new is happening regardless. People aren't going to back your project out of nowhere; they need to be reminded! Facebook posts do better when they're full of comments, so it's a great idea to ask for feedback on a post or even just pose it as a question: "Today's Kickstarter update is about our studio dog, Jeremy. Do you have an animal that helps you work? Post it in the comments!"

Facebook also loves videos, so if you have music videos or even simple performance videos of songs, upload those to Facebook, add a little video clip at the end where you talk about your crowdfunding project, and include a link to the project in the description of the video.

Instagram

Instagram is a bit of a wild card, I'm not sure how much traffic actually goes straight from Instagram to Kickstarter. However, I focus on:

- making sure people know you have a Kickstarter going on
- making it really easy to read your captions and go from your photo to your Kickstarter (like, just write out "link in bio" instead of using a hashtag, as I tend to skim past hashtags)
- being a positive influence in folks' social media feeds
- getting people invested and involved in the process behind the scenes

As we said in chapter 2, it's much preferred to make separate posts tailored to each social network, instead of just copy/pasting or linking social networks together. Twitter, Facebook, Instagram, Snapchat—they're all different services with different needs. If you use them well, they will serve you well, too.

During the last week of the project, being on top of your posts will be vital. Make sure people know how long they have to back the project! This is a great time for a livestream event to count down to the end. In promoting this livestream countdown, you're also raising awareness of the impending end of your project.

STORYTIME: THE MONTH OF GIFS!

My band's first Kickstarter was a lot of fun. Like with everything we've done, we had no idea what we were doing and just figured it out from scratch, based on what sounded fun. One of those things was animated GIFs, which are those short, looping, 3-second-video-like images you see on Twitter or Tumblr, of a cat falling over or a memorable TV show "reaction" image.

Right before the project started, I learned that I could make a GIF on my computer out of a video, and I got real, real excited. When the project hit a major milestone, my bandmate and I recorded a video together where we made surprised and excited faces (surprise and excitement are my go-to Kickstarter reactions), and I turned it into a reaction GIF.

That was fun and it pleased the Internet. At the time, GIFs were fun and novel and a little hard to make, and people were excited to see our faces because we were primarily a video-making band.

It worked and it was fun, so we kept doing it. As the project continued, we got tired of just saying, "Keep backing our project," so we decided to make a new animated GIF for every funding milestone. For every $1,000 that our project made (which was happening pretty quickly), we had a new GIF, where we were doing a new weird or funny dance. We held up the number on our hands, and added a little overlay at the bottom so people could tell what number we were celebrating.

We ended up making a couple dozen of these GIFs, and people came to expect them and get excited, even before we posted them. They'd refresh the Kickstarter page just to know when the next GIF would be coming. This was a great way to celebrate milestones without even adding stretch goals or significant additional work on our end.

Behind the scenes, this project was fun too. We genuinely enjoyed making the GIFs and coming up with new scenes and dancing, and we also learned a few lessons. My bandmate and I didn't live together, so we met up and made a handful of videos all at once so that they'd be ready to post when the time came. This is a helpful strategy for stretch goal unlocks or any social media posts: know what your needs will be ahead of time, and get your image assets ready. We learned to use our time together not to just record or make plans, but also to take photos and videos that could be shared later for our fans online.

Making GIFs was our way of building momentum that worked with our unique brand and identity, but you can find a way that works for you (or steal this one; it's worked for lots of people). I think that it worked for the following reasons, and I encourage you to find something that works for you that also hits these requirements:

- The GIFs were unique and demonstrated our quirky/cute brand in a "behind the scenes"/unfiltered sort of way.

- We were excited and positive (visibly!), so our fans were too.

- We gave them a reason to donate, because they could make a GIF happen!

- The GIFs were visual, eye-catching, and easy to understand. The number was right on there, and our tweets or Facebook posts would explain what was happening.

- We could stock up on videos when we were together, maximizing our time.

- We created a month of fun, positive, and exciting content that was consistently new, with new dances, images, and hats!

- The GIFs were free and pretty easy to make using our own resources and skills. You can see the GIFs we made here: https://doubleclicksgifs.tumblr.com/

Other projects I've seen in this category include:

- A map that unlocks new destinations as the project funds (like a video game). A little harder for a new audience to understand but excellent for a very involved audience.

- Singing or posting the names of new backers online as they back the project.

- Song videos that the audience votes on (Twitter polls, or Instagram live): "If I get to $3,000 tonight, should I sing to you about cats or hamsters?"

CHAPTER 9

Promoting an Ongoing Campaign

Hey friends, have you heard about my Patreon?
You have? Would you like to hear about it again?

An ongoing campaign is just that: it keeps on going! That means you can grow your Patreon or Bandcamp page over time. Also, you'll likely be losing followers as well, as folks' financial situations and interests change.

GETTING EARLY MOMENTUM

The easiest time to promote a crowdfunding project is right at the beginning, to build that newsworthy, exciting momentum. This means you've got to be ready when you start. Make sure the page is complete, that all the links are working, and that you are around to answer questions for the first day. Make sure it's easy to get all the information someone might need about the musical act. This is the "one click away" principle.

Just like with a one-time campaign, it's a great idea to launch your project with a single, video, song, or other big new item. Then if people like it, you can say, "If you want more, back the Patreon/Bandcamp/etc.!"

It's a good idea to be ready with examples of the types of content that followers can expect early on. Before launch, creators should have their first couple months of creations all scheduled and ready (if not complete) to demonstrate how the project will proceed.

For the launch week of this project, one way to build momentum is to have goals that are achievable. Fans love to be a part of, and celebrate, success. Reaching an early goal might result in the release of a one-time video, a cover, or even better, a participatory option, so fans can be a part of the big moment.

On day one of your project, you should post about it everywhere. If you do the work to promote your project, your fans will too! Chances are, your fans like you and want you to be happy, which is wonderful. Tell your fans what you want, and show that their support makes you happy! Through the power of social media, they can help you work toward your goal!

Promoting a Patreon

Promoting a Patreon differs from promoting a finite campaign because it doesn't really "end." There's a reason why public radio stations only fundraise at particular times in the year: there are only so many times you can ask for money before it seems like you "always" are.

The Initial Push

Just like a Kickstarter or any other project, early momentum is exciting on Patreon. This is a great use of "Patreon goals." Those give you something to celebrate as well. So before you launch a Patreon page, prepare a marketing plan for the first two or so weeks of the project, where you have eight to ten days of different content you can post to promote your project. This can be announcements, stretch goal celebrations, music videos, demos, graphics, selfies, dog pictures, livestreams—all kinds of posts you can make across all your social media that aren't just "please back my Patreon!"

Ongoing Promotion

For a lot of folks, "back my Patreon" is a pretty common thing to hear and can be easily tuned out. So, it's a good idea to have some fun places to integrate your plugs where they might actually be heard.

Good opportunities to promote Patreon include:

1. **Whenever you're posting any sort of art that was funded by your patrons.** If a music video was helped by patrons, give them a shout-out at the end and include a link in the description.

2. **When you send a newsletter to your mailing list.** Remind folks that your Patreon supporters are helping make all the great new content possible!

3. **At live shows,** especially if you can be a little subtle about it. ("This next song is one of my favorites, because we were able to make a really rad music video about it thanks to our patrons.")

4. **When you are thanking a new patron for backing the project.** Some people have "a shout-out on Twitter" as one of the rewards on Kickstarter. The double-bonus of this is that when you thank someone for backing your project publicly, it might make someone else want to be a part of it, too, to get that cool shout-out. (The downside is annoying your followers if you do this too much, so consider adding a unique joke or something fun to each post so that it adds positivity to a timeline instead of just annoyance.)

5. **When you get time to pursue a cool opportunity that your patrons funded.** Did you get to take a class? Buy a new guitar? Hire your favorite artist? Some of your fans will be very excited at the prospect of seeing the results of their donations in action!

6. **When you're close to reaching a goal.** People love an achievable goal!

COMMUNICATING WITH YOUR PATRONS

A creator should be active on their ongoing page, enough that it is evident that they are dedicating time to the community in exchange for the support provided, but it's up to you how much work you want to put into publishing on your page, and how much content you want to make that's for your backers only versus what is available to the public. It's a good idea to back a few different people on Patreon to get an idea of how often people send out updates, and what you like and don't like about that.

An ongoing project needs regular attention, because you want to keep people from cancelling their pledges. I think Patrons are more likely to stick around if you give them interesting rewards and show how their money is helping you. On the other hand, just like with anything online, Patreon pages can send out too many emails. A creator should avoid getting themselves in a situation where they send out too many messages, get annoying, and cause their subscribers to leave.

Patreon provides a few options on how to communicate with your patrons.

Posts

Most crowdfunding pages have a blog-like feed where creators can post videos, audio, stories, anything. These can be public on your page, or only available for backers, or only available for backers at a certain level. So, this is an ideal way to post your rewards, right on the page, so people can come find them when they're looking.

This feed can get overwhelmed with posts: videos, demos, stories, rewards. The most common way to deliver exclusive rewards is by making a post on the Patreon feed that is "patrons-only" to whatever level earns that particular kind of content. It's intuitive but a little overwhelming to look at a long list of posts. Fortunately, Patreon has the best use of "tags" that I've seen; below each post a creator can use words to describe the post: "MP3, reward, video, story, etc."—and then "feature" those tags on the main page so that backers can easily find what they're looking for.

Some of your fans will get an email every time you add a post that they can see, and some will only get notifications for "paid" posts. Some fans will have completely unsubscribed from notifications about these posts because they're just getting too many.

Messages

Messages are another way to contact your backers—and more often than with posts, your fans will likely get these messages right in their email inbox. Messages are good for when you need to notify your supporters of something important, like an upcoming event, or a change in pledge tiers or rewards.

Podcast Feed

Patreon also provides a podcast feed that your patrons can subscribe to (if you elect to turn it on). This is a rad but underutilized feature on the website.

Whenever you update your Patreon, via message or post, remember to keep your content positive and make sure that (most of the time) you are providing content, not just asking for something. Don't complain to your patrons that you don't have enough patrons. Thank them for existing, no matter how few they are.

Communities Outside of the Main Page

Ideally, you want your supporters to build a great community, but the crowdfunding website itself is not always the optimal place for people to get to know one another. Even pages with a lot of patrons don't get a lot of comments or people interacting with each other, though Patreon seems the ideal location for the most dedicated fans and the artist to interact. As a result, many creators choose to create their own communities outside of the Patreon page—a place to create a community that your fans are likely to use.

For example, Patreon has integration with Discord, which is a free chatroom-meets-message-board service (that you download to your phone or computer) where people can talk on various topics. Discord is popular with people in the tech and Twitch communities, and if your fans know how to use it, it's a great choice.

Patreon also integrates with Reddit, a message board/link-sharing website where folks can create communities for any subject, from video games in general to just pictures of cats with their tongues sticking out. Reddit can be a great option for communities who already use it or are willing to learn.

For my band's fan base, Facebook was the most logical option, since most people already had it, and they don't already use Reddit or Discord on a regular basis. One can create a private Facebook group and invite Patreon backers to join on their "thank you page" or via a private message or post. Facebook lets you create events within groups, which is a useful way to share tour dates, livestreams, or video premieres. We've found that our Facebook group is much more active than our Patreon page.

When creating any of these communities, creators should consider enlisting the help of knowledgeable and trustworthy fans/friends to serve as "moderators," to keep conversations on track and positive and prevent bullying or abuse.

What to Make Public, and What to Make Private?

Crowdfunding creates a community of folks invested in behind-the-scenes workings. There's a choice whenever you create something to share it publicly, or just with folks who have given you money. There's an advantage either way. When a creation is public, that means everyone can see it, it will have wider traction, and more fans will be involved. For example, my band makes all of our music videos public. If we spend a lot of time on something, we want everyone to be able to see it. On the other hand, the artist Kate Leth makes most of her comics private on Patreon, and people pay $5 or more per month just to see these great comics, which may never be released in a public place. A mix of public and private posts is normal.

Think about this: Do you want to engage young/potentially low-disposable income/non-Internet-savvy folks with this content, or just limit it? Remember that one of the benefits of Patreon is that it (ideally) affords you more time to engage with your audience online, and if you're in a phase where you want to build that audience, it may be a good idea to engage *all* of them. On the other hand, if you prioritize increasing your revenue, you may want to limit *more* of your posts to entice people on the fence to buy in.

ENDING OR PAUSING AN ONGOING CAMPAIGN

Someday, you may run out of the time or energy to run your Patreon campaign, or you may need to take a break to go on tour or have a baby. That's totally fine! The best way to do this is send a message to your Patrons and pause the campaign. (This is a built-in option for "monthly" campaigns.) Do this before you go missing or silent, if possible, so your Patrons know what's coming. As you leave, give your Patrons information on how they can keep up with you. Should they stay subscribed for when you come back, or should they follow you to another platform (social media, mailing list) where they can get updates on your next moves?

CHAPTER 10

Press Placements and Going Viral

Sell yourself to strangers on the Internet while still feeling good about it!

People spend thousands of dollars on PR agents to help promote their music. For example, a mid-level agency just contacted my band and offered to help with a three-month promotion cycle for $7,500.

This chapter is going to teach you to try to do the entry-level version of something—something that costs a lot of money to hire someone with years of experience and relationships to do.

If you've read the book thus far, you'll know that I think directly connecting with your audience is the best way to promote a crowdfunding project. You can cut out the middleman and deepen your relationship directly with your fans, which is amazing. I think that a strategy that involves direct promotion to your fans is the best use of limited time.

However, getting press is important too, even at the entry level. Press coverage can do two big things for you: (1) expose your music to new audiences, and (2) make your existing audiences excited by giving you good news to share. In my experience, the second can be even more important than the first.

There are tough things about trying to get your own press, and it's never a guaranteed thing. But I'll give you some tips.

HOW TO BE NEWSWORTHY

Indiegogo was founded in 2008, Kickstarter in 2009, and Patreon in 2013. The modern concept of crowdfunding has thus been around for a decade—which means that launching a project is not news anymore. People start crowdfunding projects every day. If you're going to be "news," it will need to be another way. Whenever a PR campaign begins, you're going to have to figure out the unique and interesting "story angle" for your musical act and your project.

It's possible your campaign will be so unique that it's worth covering. For example, Ted Leo's project was unique because he was a big name, formerly on a record label, who took a big step to make a Kickstarter campaign, and thus his project was an "industry story." Some projects are good gimmicks that are worth noting. Comedy trio, Three Busy Debras, kickstarted their way to renting a stage at Carnegie Hall because they thought it would be funny and weird, and it was.

More likely, if your crowdfunding project is newsworthy, that will be because it's successful in a big and notable way. Amanda Palmer made over $1 million, and everyone wrote about it. Smaller newspapers in the city where my band launched our project covered our campaign when we broke local goals. (Kickstarter provides useful data on their music pages to see who has the "most funded" projects by category and geographical location, so we were able to find this out.)

But if you are just running a regular project, and you haven't yet funded (or even started), you may have to find another way to be newsworthy. My strategy is something I call "launch-day media," and it requires a lot of work.

On the day you launch your crowdfunding project (and ideally, yes, it's on the same day), also launch a big piece of free art. This can be a music video, a story, a podcast, or even just a song. This big piece of art can be what news outlets write about, and your crowdfunding project can be a side note in that story. Perhaps it's not as ideal as just having someone write a story about your crowdfunding project launching, but it's much more interesting to strangers and fans alike.

Launch-day media, just like any other thing you want to get coverage for, is better if it's exciting. New. Controversial. Make this the cutest, best, most political, or most dynamic piece of art that you can think of. Think of ways to invite your fans to be part of the creation of this project.

Often, if we are launching a Kickstarter, my band will pick the song on the album that has the most interesting story, and we will make a video that has an easy angle for a lot of news outlets. Recently, we hired fifty artists to help us make a social justice-themed music video. This video was covered by feminist news outlets, local outlets, and shared by the artists who were involved.

For other bands, I've helped direct music videos that are montages of fans singing the lyrics to the single off the new album or made a simple one-take video of the title track.

Launch-day media is a gamble, because to make something newsworthy, it does need to be pretty good. A good piece of launch-day art will double as a sample to show your audience what kind of art they are supporting. It will be great content to share in your first week, even if it doesn't get covered by *Pitchfork*.

MAKE A GREAT PRESS KIT

Before you reach out to get coverage from a blog, newspaper, or any publication, make sure that you are ready for them to do some research on you. Create an electronic press kit ("EPK") on your website that includes high-resolution photos, links to your music, and a bio that gives your band's history, influences, and all the names of the members of the group and what instruments they play.

Journalists often don't have time to follow up on emails, so giving them one place to get all the information and photos they might need will increase the chances they'll write about you—and not just move on to the next thing.

MAKE A DATABASE AND MAINTAIN RELATIONSHIPS

So you have some news, and your band is easy to find and learn about. Now, you just need to find some journalists! Musical artists pass around spreadsheets full of thousands of names of reporters and music reviewers, and those are probably a good resource.

However, you should start by making your own press list. Make columns for the news outlet, its type, the name and contact information of your contact there, and links to coverage of you or similar bands. Take a look at how often they publish stories, and whether the publication is a daily blog, a weekly newspaper, or a monthly magazine. Do some research on each publication as you add it to your sheet. Do they ever post videos? Do they like interviews, or do they just announce local shows? The more you know about each potential press contact, the more you can tailor your pitch to their needs, saving everyone some time.

Once you have a spreadsheet, start filling it up by adding everyone who has ever written about your music. If a gig was mentioned in the local paper, see who wrote the story, and put them on your list. Google yourself, and find any news stories that happened before you had an awesome spreadsheet. Now you're well on your way!

Find the right person to contact. Sometimes, it can be tricky to figure out who exactly you should be emailing at a publication. Some news outlets mostly work with freelancers, and others are all just one guy writing a cool blog. But much of the time, stories are going to come from writers, not from the editor-in-chief handing them out (even though that's what happens in Spider-Man). Start by finding a story—a specific article that is similar to the one you want to pitch: a musical act at a similar level to you (there may be different people covering Beyoncé than the local open mic scene), or an article about the kinds of things you write songs about. Find the author; that's your guy! If you can click on their name, that will often lead you to a page that collects their articles.

First of all, make sure they have recent articles. Turnover is high in journalism. If they do, see if the page has a contact email. If so, you just struck gold! Hooray!

If that doesn't work, drop that person's name into Google, and do some investigation. Maybe they have their email address in their Twitter profile or on their own writing portfolio website. Note that it's often considered unprofessional to send press queries to people's Twitter DMs or personal Facebook pages, so think twice before doing that.

If you still can't find an email address for the person you want to contact, go to the "contact us" page of the publication, and find the closest thing there. Maybe that's a music editor, or maybe they have just a generic "contact us" form. That can still work. You may still want to include the name of the writer you're trying to contact when you eventually send a query. It's harder to ignore something personally addressed.

Once you've done all that sleuthing just to find an email address (or if you gave up after step 1), do you see why I told you to keep all of your information one click away? If you're hard to contact, people just aren't going to do it.

RESEARCH NEW POTENTIAL COVERAGE

It's much easier to get coverage by targeting specific folks who might be interested in your act than sending a big faceless email to a thousand-name press list. Reporters get hundreds of emails a day, and one thing that can make you stand out, in addition to a compelling story and a professional email, is knowing who you're talking to.

- Google your friends in other bands and your musical heroes. Who writes about them? Find the specific reporters who cover your genre and/or your level of artist.

- Find your local and hyper-local news outlets. There may be a newspaper in your town—maybe even one in your neighborhood.

- Think beyond newspapers and magazines. Tons of amateur and professional bloggers, YouTube review shows, and podcasts are looking for guests (and attention!). Just make sure you watch or listen to the show before you submit to it, to make sure you're a good fit and not wasting people's time.

- Ask your fans how they find out about new music and art.

- Look to outlets that don't usually cover music but might cover something else that your band is involved in—possibly the content of your lyrics, your town, or something about the identities of the members of your musical act.

- Look at instrument and genre-specific websites! The more specific, the more they may be willing to look at what you have (for example: ukulele magazines, women-focused hard rock podcasts, jazz vocalists, etc.).

- Check out some relevant hashtags on Instagram and Twitter and see who writes about stuff like yours. Maybe you could build a relationship with them, or maybe they have a website (examples: #feministmusic, #nerdmusic, #sciencesongs, #ukulele).

- When you're reading the websites that you like, scroll around and read carefully to see if they get their information from somewhere else. Sometimes, reporters for big blogs get their "tips" from a large collection of tiny websites elsewhere on the Internet. You can also find this by finding writers on Twitter/Facebook and seeing who they follow. Do some sleuthing and see if there is a little blogger who may be easier to get in touch with than the top-echelon people.

WRITE A PRESS RELEASE

A press release is basically a news story that provides all the information a reporter might need to write about a particular piece of news. This typically includes the nitty-gritty details, such as date and time, in addition to some helpful flavor, like quotations and photos. There is a lot of advice, and there are many books, on how to write good press releases. Examples are coming later in this chapter.

My main advice for you on a press release is to provide all the information a reporter needs; use correct grammar, spelling, and punctuation; and keep it as short as you can.

Press releases should include links to videos, music, and photos, if those things are relevant. Don't attach photos or anything to the email that you send unless specifically asked to do so. Speaking from experience as a reporter, our computers were slow, and our hard drives and inboxes were tiny. Please don't make the problem worse.

HOW TO SEND A GREAT EMAIL AND A GREAT FOLLOW-UP EMAIL

In most cases, when you contact a member of the press, you shouldn't just copy/paste your press release into the same email you send to 400 folks and call it a day. Unless it's an incredible press release or a slow news day, that message likely won't be in the top 10 percent of interesting emails that person has received that day.

WHEN to send your email: In an ideal world, you'd have your launch-day media and all of the information about your project ready a good month before you launch your project. You could contact magazines six to eight weeks before launch, newspapers and podcasts two to three weeks, blogs one to two weeks, and everything else in a schedule that you think makes sense. In reality, you may not be that organized, so just send your first email as soon as you have a real sample of music to show (don't send an email with just the "concept" of a new single), and send a follow-up email once your project or video is live and ready to share.

HOW to send your email: Personalize your email with a short introduction, give the absolute shortest version of your news, provide your contact information and timeline, and then, now that you have an introduction, paste the press release at the bottom of your email, with all of its wonderful links and information included.

Once you've sent the email, mark it off your list, and set yourself a reminder to follow up in one or two weeks. Keep in mind your target might be a busy reporter, or a podcaster only doing a passion project as their free time permits. Either way, they might not be able to answer you right away, so don't be pushy.

Hello Katie!

Your contact was shared with me by Lara Kirk, who has covered our band for *Billy Magazine* in the past. I'm in the Bakersfield band "Ghoul Gang." We have a feminist music video launching Monday that I'd love to share with you.

"Death Before Income Inequality" is a frustrated feminist anthem about gender roles.

https://youtu.be/ClhgfdakfdiankJ9VQI - that video goes public Monday morning at 6 a.m. Pacific!

The video for the song is made up of 50 illustrations, each created by a different woman or non-binary artist, including award-winning author Burfa Dragon.

Thank you for your time, and please let me know if I can help in any way if you're interested in sharing!

— Dara Stone, Ghoul Gang

Fig. 10.1. Sample Press Email

PRESS RELEASE: FEBRUARY 13

Ghoul Gang releases new feminist song "Death Before Income Inequality"

Ghoul Gang, a touring ghost punk band from Bakersfield, is debuting new song "Death Before Income Inequality" Monday with a music video illustrated by 50 different artists.

The lyrics of song are infused with haunting tales of ghosts and the wage gap.

I can see through the glass ceiling like you can see through me/Death before income inequality

Each phrase is accompanied by a different illustration. The artists range from award-winning author Burfa Dragon and animator Lorena McKinnon to the bandmates themselves.

"We wanted the message of the song to reach beyond our own limited experience, so we reached out to the Internet and hired 50 women and non-binary artists," said Dara Stone.

"Death Before Income Inequality" is the latest single from the forthcoming Ghoul Gang album, *You're Never Alone with Your Friends*. This will be the band's first full-length album. Starting Monday morning 2/13, Ghoul Gang is raising funds for the new album on Kickstarter, where fans can pre-order the CD and other rewards.

[YOUTUBE VIDEO link]

[LINK TO IMAGES: with captions and credits]

Fig. 10.2. Sample Press Release

INTERVIEW WITH MUSIC CRITIC DAVID GREENWALD

David Greenwald is a music critic, culture journalist, and photographer, serving as a music critic and reporter for the **Oregonian.** *He founded the* **Rawkblog,** *and also worked at* **Billboard** *and the* **Los Angeles Times.**

What work should a band do before they reach out to a reporter?

I think you really have to have your materials together. People are going to have a hard time writing about you if you don't have a decent press photo, and if your bio doesn't have basic information.

Just having that simple thing of a decent press photo that's easy to find and get the copyright information on, that's really basic and important. Aside from that, you should have your music available to listen to, have at least a short bio so someone can understand what's going on and who your group is, and a couple recommended "if you like..." items so we can understand what your music is like. Those, to me, are the very basics to get the email out.

What makes a crowdfunding project worth covering as a journalist?

Unfortunately, I don't think most people are looking at Kickstarter or Patreon as stories.

When I wrote about projects in 2014, it was because they were so successful, and Kickstarter and Patreon was a newer idea so there was a novelty factor. It was a new kind of story for readers to learn about.

I don't know that is as much the case anymore. To stand out, you'd have to have a really successful campaign, or something a little bit different.

The success is something that people are always looking for. They can ask, "Why is this group doing so well?" or "What's special about them?". Success draws in press.

This is why you should share your "wins." If you are having success, if you're booking shows, if you're getting a million views on YouTube, these are the kinds of things that make it easy for people to write about you. Especially bloggers and journalists at smaller websites who want to get on the train and share something that's already becoming popular, because then it gets traffic onto their website or their blog. There is the ulterior motive of people who want to cover something that will be popular for them as well.

How can a band make a "newsworthy" pitch? What is a good thing that someone would actually want to write about?

You just have to have an interesting story. I know this is something that musicians hear all the time, and it can be really hard to come up with. What distinguishes you? It could be anything from a group that's independent who did well by themselves, to an interesting genre, or something that's unusual for the city it's in.

As hard as it is, I think as a band or any kind of creator, you really have to think about that. Ask your friends, ask your colleagues, ask a publicist. The thing that makes your work special is what journalists are looking for in an email. They're looking for a shortcut to tell them that this is a great story!

Is it a good idea to launch a single during your Kickstarter to get some coverage that way?

I think that's great. Songs are kind of the currency right now. We've returned back to the 1950s or '60s era of the single being the king of things, and so yeah, I think if you can launch some music—a song or a video and that goes with the Kickstarter—that's the perfect thing. You can say, "Hey, here's this song," and the Kickstarter becomes almost like a pre-order. "If you want more, you can come in and check us out and give us money."

But if you just launch the Kickstarter without a sample of the music, then you're just saying, "We're gonna do this thing, and we don't really have any kind of evidence to confirm to you that you should give us your money."

Certainly, it depends on the artist and the fan base, but as far as the pitch to journalists or new audiences, it's gonna be much stronger if you have a song or a video, or even tour dates. Something you can use to sweeten the deal.

Who should a band reach out to at a publication, and when?

If there is a publication you like or a writer you like, just email them directly. The writer level is best. Alternatively, if you can figure out who the music editor is or someone who might be in a position to assign stories, that's good too. You don't want to go all the way up to the editor-in-chief of the newspaper, or someone like that.

As far as when: as soon as possible! People need as much time as possible with that heads-up. I know we're no longer really in the world of the three-month album cycle anymore, but people still have print deadlines. Even if it's a news story with less lead time or a premiere, you don't have far in advance. A couple days' heads-up is ideal. Every hour counts, because writers get hundreds of emails a day, and they really need as much time as they can get to prepare your story.

What makes a musician someone you wanted to write about, if they don't have a manager or PR agent?

Personally, I come from writing and blogging about indie rock and undiscovered bands, and that's what I'm passionate about. I was always looking to read emails that came directly from musicians, because that's what was more interesting to me than something from a PR company. I was very willing to listen to the music and see if I heard something there that I thought was special—something that I could help spotlight.

I think the most important thing is to be professional, look at some examples of what a PR email looks like, include your information, be respectful of the writer's time by being concise and presenting it in an organized way, and don't make the mistake of thinking you're making friends with this journalist.

I don't need eight paragraphs of information about how you drove across the country and blah blah blah. Just tell me who you are, show me the music. The most important thing is to be concise and professional. Just put together a really good email, wait one or two weeks, send a follow-up, and if you don't get any response after that, you can move on with your life and trust that the editor has just deleted it and moved along.

From there, I don't think it matters necessarily if you have a manager or PR or not.

Working with PR professionals can help get you in the door because writers are going to have existing relationships with publicists and be more attentive to those emails. Having that PR endorsement is a co-sign already that this is going to be a serious thing, from a professional band, who might be worth listening to. But you know, at the end of the day, it's all just emails.

How do you feel about press releases versus more casual emails? What makes a good one, and what makes a bad one?

I think you can do both in the same email. I always really like the emails where the publicist says, "Hey, here's what's up, here's the link to dive right in, here's the full release below if you want to read it and get all that information."

There are some writers who are almost going to copy/paste the press release into their article, whereas other people want to make a decision about whether they like it or if it's interesting before they go through and spend five minutes reading the whole release.

I'd say, do a hybrid where you put the real information up front. Here's the YouTube link, here's the MP3, here's whatever the main gist of the email is. And then paste the full release with all the information that they can look at it, if you want to.

What makes a good band website, from a press perspective?

Most musicians do not have a functional press kit page on their website, and I don't understand it! You should have one page, and it should have your bio and your photos and a list of who's in the band, and what instruments they play. When I go to the site, I'm looking to get lyrics or liner note-type things, so when I write something, I can say, "This person plays guitar on track 3," and get that right.

Not everyone wants to do that fact checking, but I would say, really make sure that basic information is there.

Should bands invite press to live shows? How and when should they do this?

It's funny because this industry has changed so much, but back in the '90s or '00s, most critics or reporters were going to shows five nights a week. That's how you'd really learn about local bands: by being invited to that show, and checking out the musicians, and seeing if it's something you want to write about.

I don't know if that's as important now, and I don't think there's the budget at most publications to be sending people out to shows all the time. But certainly, anytime you have a show and there's local press, you tell the writers, "Hey, come to my show, and I'll put you on the list."

It never hurts to do that, and if you can get people out to the show, hopefully they'll review it. But even if they don't, it may lead to a piece later. Just getting in front of your audience, and some writers, is going to be something that's super important and advisable whenever you have a show.

What should artists do after an article goes live?

Share it on social media, because unfortunately, we live in the era where writers are constantly checking their stats. It is really helpful to us if the article gets shared, and then we can go to our editor and say, the artists shared it. That does create a weird conflict of interest zone, because you're not supposed to be promotional as a reporter, but that's the way of things. Sites that are more like someone's blog or a music-oriented site are going to be more aggressive than somewhere like the *New York Times* in looking for those shares.

Now you have a piece of press that you can use in your next round of emails to people. The more press you have under your belt, the more other writers are going to have that fear of missing out, and say, "Oh, I should be covering this because everybody else is writing about it." People are always looking for that co-sign, especially writers, because if something is coming without a reputation—if it doesn't have these markers that people are looking for to see if something is serious, or something that's about to break out and become more popular—it can be harder to write about it, which is a bummer but it's a reality.

I don't know if you can build a ten-year career around this, but in the case of a one-month/three-month press cycle, every article should be a stepping-stone to try to get the next article.

What are your biggest pet peeves—what should musicians *not* do?

I'll give you a few. First, too many emails. Send one, send the follow-up, and then you're done. Anything beyond that and you're kind of being a pest. Three emails, tops.

Another is reaching out to people on Facebook or places that are not professional channels. Most writers really hate that.

Another is sending an email with attachments as opposed to links to your photos and your media.

What else should people know when trying to promote their band?

We're all in our own little world of what makes sense at our publication. It is really important to be aware and do some homework of, like, what's gonna be different at an alt weekly, versus a national magazine, versus this website. This is where a publicist can be really helpful to say, "Here's what's going to make sense for this type of publication, and we can tailor it." A really good publicist is not someone who's just sending out 2,000 emails and following up, because you can do that. That's just having a spreadsheet and sending out emails. What a really good publicist is going to do is look for those opportunities and say, "Oh, you're this kind of band, and these three publications would be a fit, or this brand would be a fit, or we can get you in front of these influencers and then we can go from there," and try to build the story of the band, and build up the awareness of it, and find the right audience.

The other good advice that I heard was on a Tim Ferriss podcast. He said when he was trying to launch *The Four-Hour Workweek*, back in the day, was, "I don't need to have 100 articles out. I need to have three articles from the top five publications that my audience reads." If you can get those one, two, or three pieces of attention from the right people, that really expands the reach and creates the FOMO: Fear Of Missing Out. It's way better to have that one big thing than the twenty medium things. At the same time, someone will premiere a track on *Pitchfork*, and it will get less attention than on another, less cluttered site because it's on a list of 500 things that came out that day.

It's all just about figuring out where's the audience and what are the best ways to reach them.

THINKING BEYOND THE PRESS

Word of mouth has always been an important way for people to find out about art. With the world of social media exploding, however, there's a fun new word for a special kind of word-of-mouth: *influencers*. Influencers are "famous people," "celebrities," or even just normal humans with a lot of followers on the Internet. In previous generations, they may have been called "tastemakers."

Influencers are also just anybody who has an audience, which can be almost all of us these days. When you launch a project, it's great to tell all of your friends to tell their friends about your project. It's especially important to reach out to your friends who are influencers, and it is usually worth doing this in a more professional way.

First of all, who are your "influential" friends and connections? They are anyone!

- other bands
- venue owners
- festival runners
- accompanists
- teachers
- writers
- people who tweet a lot
- comic and other visual artists
- authors
- poets
- inspirational speakers
- fashionable teens
- any professional content creators

These are your friends you went to elementary school with, people you may have met at conventions or work, or even friends whose work you admired online and then developed a friendship with. My band makes sci-fi music and, as a result, has a lot of friends who are sci-fi actors or authors. We perform at game stores and make friends with the owners, as well as the people who make board games.

Hopefully, you're reading this well before your Kickstarter launches, because you should do some work building up karma before you ask your influencer friends for help. Some people would just call this "mutual friendship," but it's also a great strategic move for your music! Here's why:

When you ask your content-creator friends for help, you're counting on them to believe in a "rising tide lifts all boats" mentality—and you should believe that, too. There are some genres or groups of performers who are very competitive, who don't promote one another's music or shows because they think people will "steal their audience." Don't be like this. My band has been lucky to have a great community of musicians around us from the very beginning, bringing us on tour, giving us advice, and sharing fans on the Internet. I started a Facebook group with small number of "nerdy musicians" where we give one another advice about software and touring locations, and ask for help promoting big projects. I create playlists on my band's YouTube page featuring other musicians in our genre. My band hosts an online show each month and features a special guest, another musical artist, to introduce them to our audience.

A community of artists is essential to happiness in an artist career, so have a generous spirit, and definitely share your audience with your friends. Listen to their music, read their articles, back them on Patreon—and share all of these things with your fans. Be an eager and outspoken fan of your friends. It's good to do this for each other all year round, by the way. When someone has a free piece of content out (a new comic, video, story), your fans may be more likely to check it out than something that costs money.

When you ask your friends for help, it's not guaranteed, of course. You never know what their policies are on sharing their friend's stuff, or even what their week or month is like. But at least you won't seem like a freeloader or a jerk who asks for help but never gives it.

How to Ask Your Friends for Help

1. **Make sure you're doing the work.** You need to be promoting yourself so much that your friends have noticed. If it seems like you're just asking them to do the work for you, that's not a great vibe.

2. **Make it easy.** Give your friends a direct link to send out to their followers. When we get "asks" like this from buddies of ours, they even sometimes give us sample text we could put in our Twitter post. That's super helpful.

3. **Be kind and personal.** Avoid sending one big email to every single person you know. You don't need to write each one individually, but it does need to be thoughtful. And if you send a mass email, make sure to put everybody in the "bcc" line. It's rude to send out everybody's email addresses to everyone else.

4. **Send your "ask" at a good time of day.** Your friends are busy people and you're asking them for a favor, so if they follow through on your request, they may do so immediately. It's thus good to send your email at a time of day where it would be most helpful to your project. Generally, this is early in the morning on a weekday, rather than late at night or on a weekend.

5. **Don't over-ask.** Put your influencer friends on your press list, and check off when you've contacted them so you don't do it too much. Make sure you have a good feel for your relationship. There are some bands who I will promote all the time no matter what, and my best friend is a musician with whom I am constantly trading favors (like, "Please comment on my Instagram so I don't look desperate"). But there are some people I'll just reach out to once per year, because they don't—and don't need to—ask me for anything in exchange.

6. **Be direct.** Everybody's got a pet peeve, and this one is mine: I don't like it when somebody mentions me in a tweet, obviously intending that I retweet it. (Example: "I have loved touring with people like @ghoulgangmusic this year, and we can do more of it, if you back us on Patreon! Patreon.com/notverysubtle"). I'd much rather just receive a direct email that has all the information I need. I don't want to feel like people think my support is implied or like I'm being manipulated. That being said, if we discuss it beforehand, a tweet like that is totally fine with me.

7. **Give them something fun to share.** Just like with the press, your friends may be more excited to share a free piece of art (a song or video) than just a link to a fundraiser.

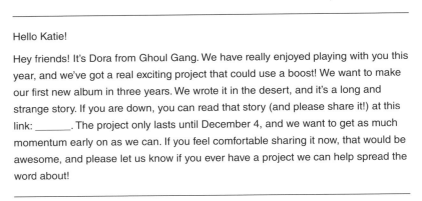

Hello Katie!

Hey friends! It's Dora from Ghoul Gang. We have really enjoyed playing with you this year, and we've got a real exciting project that could use a boost! We want to make our first new album in three years. We wrote it in the desert, and it's a long and strange story. If you are down, you can read that story (and please share it!) at this link: _____. The project only lasts until December 4, and we want to get as much momentum early on as we can. If you feel comfortable sharing it now, that would be awesome, and please let us know if you ever have a project we can help spread the word about!

Fig. 10.3. Sample: Asking a Friend for Help

PART IV

Following Through
When It's Over: Next Steps

CHAPTER 11

From Funding Campaign to Product Launch: Fulfilling Your Project

It's over

(no it's not)

(not even a little bit)

In some ways, once you have that money, the Kickstarter project is "over." But in other ways, it's very, very not! In addition to making your product and sending it out to your fans, you've also got to keep everybody in the loop while you're creating, and ideally have a big launch for your piece of art. All of that communication and success will build up goodwill for the next project—whether it's another crowdfunding project, a tour, or a build to something else!

SAY THANK YOU!

The absolute most important thing to do once your project funds, ends, or hits a goal is to say thank you. Thank your backers publicly and often—and don't forget to put it on the page! You can't just say it on Twitter. Put it in an update and/or a blog post. Fans feeling the gratefulness from creators is just as important as them knowing about the project in the first place!

Offer a catch-up mechanic for people who missed the project, like a link for pre-order, and a place to sign up for your mailing list.

GET YOUR MONEY

Services like Kickstarter collect payment information throughout your project and then charge once, at the end of the project. Patreon collects money on the first of the month. Inevitably, since the charge is happening days or weeks after the backer has pledged their money, some of your backers' pledges aren't going to work. Maybe their card got stolen or changed, information got entered incorrectly, or possibly they simply don't have the money. This is awkward and strange to deal with. Fortunately, most of the platforms (including Patreon and Kickstarter) will send a message to your backer letting them know that their charge has failed. Some people will fix their payment method during the "grace period," and some of them won't. If you feel comfortable doing so, you can track down the backers whose pledges have failed. Some of them may not be aware and could use the nudge.

Because of those bounced pledges and fees, you should ready yourself for a little bit of "sticker shock" when the payment finally hits your inbox. (This will be a few days to two weeks after your backers have been charged.) That beautiful number you saw on the last day of your project is not going to be what you see; it will be less. Possibly, much less. That's expected, and hopefully the spreadsheets earlier helped you build in a "safety zone" to plan for it. If not, keep reading, we'll get to "what happens when something goes wrong."

THE SURVEY: GETTING THE INFORMATION YOU NEED TO FULFILL YOUR PROMISES

When you buy something (say, a T-shirt) on the Internet, frequently, you give your shipping address and shirt size before you pay. This is not the case on all crowdfunding platforms, which has given rise to the "Crowdfunding Survey." This is a form, usually built into a crowdfunding platform, that backers fill out to give all the information needed to get them their rewards. On Kickstarter, the creator needs to build this survey within the website and send it out after the project has funded, and backers have been charged. The survey is one of the places where things can go wrong, so be careful when you create them! I've found that it's surprisingly difficult to get people to respond to emails or fill out surveys, even when it's the only way they will get something they've already paid for. Chasing people down for information is a little bit like chasing down homework from graduating seniors. It's a good idea to be prepared to send out a really excellent survey that will get you all the information you need in one fell swoop. It's also a good idea to make your survey concise and easy to fill out, so people don't get overwhelmed and leave, thinking they will "come back to it." (Spoiler: they won't.)

Here's information you need from the survey.

Contact Information

You need to be able to send your rewards. That means you need a mailing address for rewards, of course, but you should also ask for an email address. A surprising number of folks connect their Kickstarter/Facebook/Patreon accounts to an email address that they seldom check—either an old address or something they set up specifically for "spam." That means if you send a link to a digital album or a question about a custom reward to the email address your fan has on file with the crowdfunding software, that fan may never receive it. (This same phenomenon is the reason some people will never fill out their Kickstarter surveys.)

Specifications

Take a look at your crowdfunding page, all of your updates, and your reward levels, and then make a list of each "reward level" or "tier" and all of the things those fans will be receiving. Some rewards may require questions: shirt size, whose name you should thank in the credits, what special song they'd like you to cover, etc. Some don't, like a CD. Assume this is your one chance to request information and do it!

Some nice touches:

- Put a link to a sizing chart for whatever kind of shirt you're printing, if you're asking for a shirt size from fans. Sizing varies wildly from company to company, and you can usually find a chart online by Googling the exact model of shirt that your vendor is making for you.
- Don't assume that fans remember what they ordered. Spell it out in the question. Instead of "What is your song request?" ask something like, "With your reward, you can request one of Ghoul Gang's songs for us to play in our special spaceship livestream concert. What is your request?"

Follow-Up Information

Help your fans follow you in the next step of your project or career. Include a box where they can select whether they want to sign up for your email list, and whether they'd like to be contacted about the opportunity to buy more merch from you.

A note on changing addresses: some people are going to move, in between when you ask them for their shirt size and when you send it out, but you're still going to need that shirt size before you can ship them the shirt. Most crowdfunding platforms have accounted for this. There is an option to allow address changes in your survey, so fans can fill out the survey as early as possible, and then you can send a warning to fans later (sometimes months later!) that you are about to ship their products, and you need them to update their addresses within the system.

Alternate Fulfillment Services

Since crowdfunding became popular, services such as BackerKit, PledgeManager, and others have cropped up to help creators fulfill their projects easier. Many of them also provide options for fans to buy *add-ons*—additional items that were not initially part of their orders (discussed later this chapter).

In situations where you want to offer something that your platform doesn't have the infrastructure for, these fulfillment services can be helpful systems. Unfortunately, they also sometimes require fans to create a second account on a separate website to give you their shipping information and product preferences, and this creates a new tier of complication in trying to track down your fans. When your customers have to do more work, you have to do more work to teach them how to do it. So, having a fulfillment service to work with may not, in fact, "simplify" the process. Plus, they cost money. So do your research and proceed with caution. Crowdfunding services have gotten better and better at making easy-to-use systems, so external fulfillment services are less and less necessary.

Stragglers

One week, two weeks, three months, even a year after your project is done, some of your backers may have still not filled out their surveys. Maybe they got busy, maybe they lost the password for their email account. It's better to find them early, because sometimes these backers will come to a show, or send you an email months, or even years in the future asking for their rewards. This gets difficult when you don't have that CD or T-shirt anymore! After about a month, I tend to start hounding these backers everywhere I can so I can get them checked off my list and avoid having to deal with it when the project is long done. Frequently, I can find the backers on Facebook or email and send them a message like this:

> Hey Janice! It's Dara from Ghoul Gang. We're ordering the custom polar fleece vests that you ordered on our Kickstarter page, and we need to know your size! We sent out a survey through Kickstarter on March 3, but we haven't heard from you. Please log in to your Kickstarter account to fill out that survey, or simply reply to this message with your shipping address and the size of vest you'd like. If we don't hear from you by June 6, we will order you a size XL. If we don't get your address by August 19, we will not be able to send you your reward. Please get back to us as soon as you can!

No matter how many times I message stragglers, some of them don't show up until the week after we've shipped our rewards. They'll see pictures of other people enjoying their CDs and T-shirts and demand, "WHERE IS MINE?" Being in customer service like this is my least favorite part of crowdfunding. However, these fans did give you money, so you need to bring out your postal scale again and ship them their rewards. People may keep showing up even years in the future, so don't get rid of the "extra" items you ordered for them, though I do recommend setting a deadline in your follow-up emails (like in the Ghoul Gang message above).

ADD-ONS

Add-ons are a crowdfunding-specific concept that was created by folks who have run projects. If a fan wants to build their own à la carte reward, such as an additional CD or T-shirt, an "add-on" system allows them to send you more money in exchange for this new, custom level. Add-ons do add a level of complication to the fulfillment process, so if this is your first time or you already have a lot on your plate, it may be a good idea to not buy into an add-on option. However, if you do, there are a few options to do it. Services like BackerKit and PledgeManager that will run an add-on system for you in exchange for (a pretty large amount of) money. These can be worth it if your fans buy a lot of add-ons. If you want to run it yourself, you can set up a store on PayPal, Square, SquareSpace, or your own website, and send out a link to that store with your crowdfunding survey for folks to use.

Indiegogo has a built-in system to set up a store for backers and for people who missed your project, after project ends, and those could be used for add-ons.

Add-ons seem pretty simple but add a lot of complication to a project (and your spreadsheets), so think your plan all the way through, and proceed with caution.

MAKE YOUR THING (YOUR ART AND YOUR ITEMS!)

This isn't a book about how to make a music video or record an album, so I won't tell you how to do that. However, the most important thing to do after a project has funded is to stay on schedule and communicate with everyone involved. Have a calendar marked with due dates for all of your contractors (artists, CD and Vinyl replicators, mastering engineers, crafters, shirt printers), and follow up with everyone as time passes. Make a list of every step in your process (and every dollar you spend!), and refer to it constantly. Be clear with your expectations when you hire people, especially friends or fans, and keep yourself on track as well. And all the while, keep your backers up-to-date with what's going on. If you get new photos, new mixes, new designs—use a Kickstarter update to send everyone a picture! Folks signed up to get behind-the-scenes access, so keep them updated.

FULFILLMENT

Physical Items

Sending out physical rewards requires a lot of logistical juggling. If you're a person who likes spreadsheets, you can import the information from your crowdfunding surveys into software like Excel or Google Sheets (which is free). You'll get a lot more information than you need, and you can narrow it down and (if you're good at manipulating spreadsheets) do the math on how many shirts of what size you'll need, how many CDs to order—just like any other online store fulfillment.

Create a packing list for each reward. Just like when creating a survey, look over your whole crowdfunding page. Make sure you haven't forgotten about a stretch goal or some promise you made in an update in the heat of the project. The most surefire way to lose the faith of your fans is to not give them what they paid for.

The trickiest part, when it comes to fulfilling physical items, is packing and shipping them. You can hire people to do this for you, through various crowdfunding fulfillment houses, but if you want to save money and do it yourself, here are some tips.

Packing

Use bubble mailers for CDs, stickers, pins, and small items. They're light and easy to address, and keep products relatively safe. Spring for bubble mailers that are good quality. The cheapest ones available on Amazon may fall apart, and you don't want to be in the situation of sending out everything twice.

T-shirts, tote bags, and other soft things can be sent in "poly mailers." These soft products can make great shipping materials to wrap CDs and fragile items in.

For posters, if you're using USPS, expect that large envelopes will be folded and torn. I've seen failure with "flat" envelope packing, and success with packing posters in tubes, for the security of the art.

For other bulky items, do the calculation to see if a "flat rate" box from the postal service will save you money when shipping a box of rewards. Usually, it won't, but if you have something heavy to pack, give it a try. Generally, it's going to be cheaper to know the dimensions of the stuff you need to ship and to order packing materials in bulk online than to try to find them last minute at a store.

Shipping

You have the option of bringing a big pile of addressed envelopes to the post office. This will take a lot of time for you and them, but you can do it. Depending on the number of packages, however, there are better options.

Many U.S. post offices have automated machines where customers can calculate and print their own postage based on the size and weight of the package. If you have many packages of the same size and weight (a bunch of CDs, for example), a post office employee or that machine can help print stamps of a certain value in bulk.

Even better: for a monthly fee, services like Endicia and Stamps. com allow creators to print postage at home and just drop off packages at the post office already paid for (see chapter 4). Endicia does not require that you buy a special scale; you can measure packages using a kitchen scale or any cheap small scale.

Tips:

- Calculate postage before your project launches. International postage can be much, much more than you might expect.
- Make sure to use the "package" option, and not "envelope," when shipping anything thicker than a letter, or your package will be returned to you.
- Printing postage from Endicia or Stamps.com is printing money. Don't mess it up!
- Order extra ink cartridges as a backup if you're printing lots of postage.
- Services such as Endicia allow creators to print large sheets of stamps instead of single postage labels, which may be faster than individually importing addresses into your software.
- Many label companies (like Avery) have free software that will input addresses from a spreadsheet to easily mail-merge into a sheet of labels.

Digital Items

It can seem easy. A digital reward can just be emailed to your fans, right? But sending big files across the Internet is a little more complicated than it seems like it should be.

There aren't perfect, free solutions for sending out digital items. I'd love to be able to just make them appear in everybody's iTunes, Google, Amazon, or wherever they already listen to music, but there are a few usable options:

- **Dropbox:** You can upload your album to Dropbox and send a link to all of the fans who ordered it. You can also post a Dropbox link in an update on your crowdfunding page, accessible only to backers at the "digital album" level or above, and that link will be available forever, which is very convenient.

  However, if the file is too big or too many people access it, this could overload your Dropbox account, and suddenly freeze up on you. Do the math to be sure that your Dropbox (or Google Drive, or other file-sharing service) can handle the size of the file and the number of people (bandwidth) who will be accessing the file.

- **Link on your website:** If your website has a way to upload files, that could be a good alternative to a Dropbox file. If you know how, you can create a pretty, password-protected page on your website with links to all kinds of digital rewards. This also has the benefits listed above for Dropbox, and the same concerns. You don't want your fans to crash your website.

- **Bandcamp download code:** Bandcamp is a great resource for independent artists. You can generate download codes for your album, and send them out to your backers for free, or inexpensively. The downside of this, of course, is that you'll have to individually send a download code to each backer, and unless you have a computer whiz on your team who can help automate this process, it can take a long time. The upside is that Bandcamp provides downloads in all kinds of formats (which is a plus for people who love large, lossless recordings), and any fans who already have a Bandcamp account can add the album to their library to download whenever they want, even if their computer crashes and takes all their music with it.

- **Indiehitmaker** has a "Dropkick" service that will mail a download of your album to your fans and register the sale to SoundScan. This service costs money depending on the number of albums you need to fulfill, but if you want a hands-off option, it might be worth exploring. **ArtistShare** has built-in album release options, and **BackerKit** also can host up to a certain size of digital file.

Custom Rewards

Custom rewards take longer than rewards that are the same for everybody, but they can be a lot of fun, if you organize the process. The first step to an easily fulfilled custom reward is a good survey. Hopefully, you can get all the information you need from the questions in your survey to go ahead and make your reward. If not, be sure to ask for a good direct email address so that you can communicate with your fan directly.

- **Be nice!** This isn't just a "store-type" transaction. Your fan gave a lot of money to be able to communicate with you, so be friendly, and be on time. Set realistic expectations as to when you'll be communicating and delivering your reward.

- **Guard your time.** Backers are busy people and may not reply to you promptly. I recommend setting deadlines for feedback and strict guidelines as to how you will create the reward, from the very beginning. If it's a piece of art, make it clear how much direction and feedback the backer will be allowed to have. If you ask a question and the answer is necessary to fulfilling the reward, give a hard deadline your fan needs to meet in order to get their reward.

- **Be on time.** Custom rewards are often the most time-consuming to fulfill, which means they can be the last ones finished and ready to ship out. However, these are the backers who gave you the most money, so they should not be receiving their rewards later than anyone else. If there are custom physical items that will take a long time to create, either hold off fulfilling the rest of your project until the rewards are finished, or ship these "custom item" backers their regular rewards at the same time as everyone else, and the custom items later. I once had to wait over a year to get a comic book I'd Kickstarted, just because I had leveled up my pledge to support at a higher level with an additional reward. By the time I got my comic book, it had been out to the public for months, and I wasn't excited about it anymore. I didn't even really feel good about the creators anymore. Be nice to your backers. Give them what they asked for, and do it on time!

RELEASING AN ALBUM THROUGH CROWDFUNDING

Other books can talk more to the state of the industry. It's said that the album is dying, the single is back, and that no one buys music anymore—all of that may be true. Here's what you need to know to promote an album that you made via crowdfunding.

- **Give your backers first priority on access to your art.** By the time your album is out to the world, your backers should have their digital and physical rewards in hand.

- **Don't lose momentum.** An audience is most excited about an album when they first hear it. This is when they'll be most likely to talk and post about it. When this happens, their friends may be curious and get FOMO (fear of missing out)—and a creator should exploit this! I think Kickstarter backers should get their albums before the rest of the world, but not *too early.* If your superfans get the album two weeks before it comes out, they might not be talking about it anymore when the actual release date rolls around.

  If an album releases on Friday the 10th, I recommend shipping rewards so that they arrive on the 5th to 8th, and releasing the digital album to backers on the 7th or 8th. These people who invested in you can get early access and feel cool, but the momentum built by your project isn't lost, and your fans who missed the crowdfunding project don't feel like they are being punished.

  Releasing the album at the same time to everyone also allows a creator to maximize their chances of "charting" on *Billboard*. Labels or services such as Indiehitmaker can help bands register their crowdfunding pre-sales for SoundScan (which is the service *Billboard* uses for its charts). Bandcamp has this chart submission capability built into the platform, and independent artists can pay Indiehitmaker to help get their pre-orders registered for the charts. There are specific rules to be eligible that those services can help set you up with, but generally to make this happen, artists will need to prove that an album has been paid for and delivered to a backer and provide additional information, such as their postal code information along with this proof.

- **Make your album easy to listen to.** I back a ton of projects on Kickstarter. I pre-order albums on Bandcamp, and I support dozens of musicians on Bandcamp. But the truth is, though I am a huge fan and supporter of independent music, I mostly listen to music on Apple Music or Spotify. It's just easier. I don't have a CD player, and I don't spend the time importing my iTunes library to my phone. So when an album comes out, even if I get easy access to it on Kickstarter, I'm still not going to listen to it till it's somewhere I can stream it.

    I'm just one person, of course. I have plenty of friends who work hard to download FLAC files and import them to their hard drives, or who exclusively listen to vinyl. But my point is, your music should be accessible to all of these people. To maximize the release of your album, people need to not only be able to buy it, but also to listen to it. And if they're all listening to it at roughly the same time, that's even better. Your album may only have one moment to break into the news cycle (or even the social media cycle), so I'd optimize it as much as possible. And make sure people know to use your hashtag!

STAY IN TOUCH WITH YOUR BACKERS!

Fulfilling a crowdfunding project is a lot more than just sending out a product. When someone backs a crowdfunding project, they're doing more than just buying something from a store. They're putting faith in a creator, toward a project that may not ever exist. This goodwill and faith is the very thing that's wonderful about crowdfunding. Your fans want to be involved in the project. They don't just want to buy the CD.

So, once the project is funded and you're doing the busywork of finishing up that project, don't forget that your audience has paid for an experience, and you still need to give it to them.

For a Kickstarter-type project, updates can come monthly or more often. Send pictures from the studio, show prototypes and art, and tell stories of what you're doing and working on. You can create "backer-only" updates that create an exclusive experience for the people who invested and believed in you. So, share the good stuff. Do you have a demo of your music? Did you get a cool guest vocalist? Did you have a big realization about art?

If you think you may have trouble remembering to update your fans, give yourself a reminder—every other Monday, the first Tuesday of the month, whatever it is—to write a short post for your backers.

This staying-in-touch is not just a good thing to do for your backers; it will also be helpful for two big parts of the project: momentum when you launch your final product, and good faith when something (inevitably) goes wrong.

WHAT HAPPENS WHEN SOMETHING GOES WRONG?

The world is full of unexpected moments. Independent artists are part of the world. Unfortunately, independent artists also don't have paid time off, substitutes, or any sort of cushion to absorb those unexpected surprises. So chances are, in the course of making any project, especially with many people and moving parts involved, something is going to go wrong.

Things that have gone wrong for Kickstarters, causing the project to be unexpectedly delayed:

- There's a holiday you didn't know about in the country where your product is being made. (Watch out for Chinese New Year!)

- The band/band's family is fighting/sick/pregnant/getting married/otherwise extremely busy in an unexpected way.

- You realize you owe $25,000 in taxes and have to use Kickstarter money to pay them.

- The CD arrives, and the art is printed upside down.

- Someone runs away with the money.

- An artist completely flakes on you, or turns out to be a jerk.

- You sign yourself up to do something that is a lot harder than you think it is.

- You spill an entire diet soda into the laptop holding the only copy of your album.

There are some things that may come up that aren't good excuses to delay your project: an unnecessary vacation, even a gig. Remember, though, that your fans have already paid you, so you should treat your crowdfunded project like a job that you can't just leave. But if the problem is unavoidable, it's understandable, and you just need to be honest.

Hopefully, you've built some leeway into your timeline and budget that can absorb whatever problems arise. Ideally, you've done all the work you could before launching your project.

Tell your supporters as soon as possible. If something's gone wrong that's going to affect the project, your backers will find out about it sooner or later. If you tell them early on, it demonstrates professionalism and that you are working on it. Most of your backers will understand that you're an independent artist running a huge operation and you are doing your best. Going silent will raise suspicion and not make the problem better.

Stay positive and take the high road. Even though things aren't going according to plan, you can still be a ray of sunshine in your fans' days when your update hits the inbox. A message blaming other people is going to seem like an excuse. You are the project manager; blaming someone else doesn't make the problem disappear. Don't deny that something is wrong or get defensive. People can see through this. Be honest. It's not unusual that something went wrong; this happens with almost every project. Balance out the bad news with some good updates, keep your fans updated on how you are going to solve the problem, and make it clear that you're still working and appreciative of their support. Chances are, many of them won't even know that things are delayed, so your honesty and update will just seem like you're very on top of it.

Update #20—Ghoul Gang—July 20, 2020
Things have been delayed?

Hey everybody! We're very sorry to have to do this to y'all, but our album has been delayed and we can't quite get it back on schedule as soon as we'd like. As you know, we planned to get "You're Never Alone with Your Friends" to you in September. We were planning to be done in the studio by today, July 20. Unfortunately, last week, Dara got called away and isn't going to be able to record her parts until she returns.

We built a lot of leeway into this project, but this was an unexpected turn. Dara's been busy all year since she discovered the superpowers activated by the ghosts we met in the desert, and since the government found out about it, research projects and interviews have been complicating our recording schedule. As you know, Dara is our kickass drummer and the creator of a lot of the beatboxing sounds we need on the record, and we don't think this album would be a true "Ghoul Gang Experience" if we replaced her.

Fortunately, Dara's already rescheduled her recording dates for when she returns, so we think we should be back on track to release the album about six months late. In the meantime, we have made our flannel vests and custom Ouija boards, but those will be shipping late as well so we can send them with the CD. Speaking of which, here's the final design!

Thank you all so much for your patience, and love to Dara as she confronts her inner demon! (Literally.)

Fig. 11.1. Notice of Delay

Solve the problem without hurting your fans. How can you adjust your project without taking money away from your product? Can you delay a little bit, can you take on some work, can you ask a family member for help? Keep working until you have a solution. Many a Kickstarter has gone wrong when a creator hit an obstacle and just waited for it to go away. You've already done the magic of funding something that wasn't there before; you can solve a problem in one part of this giant machine you built.

If it's on an ongoing campaign and you need to change your reward levels because of a new situation, that's okay too! If you told your fans you'd be doing a video chat every month or three videos a week and that's not possible anymore, you just need to tell them, and update your page and reward levels accordingly. A post or message with complete information—the situation, the changes, the plan, and the timeline—will be all they need. Some people may cancel or adjust their pledges, but that is better than falling behind or ghosting on them.

GET READY FOR NEXT TIME

When the project is done and rewards are sent out, you have a wonderful community, a new connection you've built with them, and a great new work of art. Much can be gained from continuing the process you started with your project, especially if you want to do this again in the future.

Continue to update your project. Keep your backers updated on the success of the thing they made. If it's an album, tell them when you're touring it. If it won an award or charted on *Billboard*, tell your backers, and thank them for making it happen.

Update your press sheet and send thank-you emails. Did you get coverage for your project? Send thank-you emails to the journalists who wrote about you, and add their contact information to your press list.

Add fans to your mailing list. Export the data from your crowdfunding survey, and import those people into your email list. Do this with their zip codes, if you can, and you'll have a bunch more data you can use to plan tours, and send out targeted show announcement messages.

Conduct a postmortem on your campaign. Make note of what was hard to make, what was fun to make, and how long things took to create. Did money go to unexpected places? Were some rewards more popular than you expected? Could you have charged more for them? What were the perks and disadvantages of the platform? If you're anything like me, next time you launch a project, you'll have completely forgotten all of the bad parts. Write down your lessons learned so you'll be better off next time.

AFTERWORD

Well, that was more work than I expected.

I hope that crowdfunding brings you great success, joy, and satisfaction. Kickstarter, Patreon, and even tiny pass-the-hat crowdfunding campaigns have made it possible for me to spend my life making the art I want to make, and helping other people do the same. I'll be the first to admit there are downsides to the Internet, but the magic that comes from a direct relationship between creators and their communities nearly makes up for it.

Best of luck on your crowdfunding adventure! Make beautiful art!

Recommended Reading

BOOKS

Palmer, Amanda. *The Art of Asking or How I Learned to Stop Worrying and Let People Help*. New York: Grand Central Publishing, 2014.

Herstand, Ari. *How to Make It in the New Music Business: Practical Tips on Building a Loyal Following and Making a Living as a Musician*. New York: Liveright, 2016.

Zitron, Ed. *This Is How You Pitch: How to Kick Ass in Your First Years of PR*. Muskegan, MI: Sunflower Press, 2013.

WEB RESOURCES

The Roaring Crowdfund Podcast. This five-episode podcast from Berklee Online, the online school of Berklee College of Music, examines four musical acts, and tracks their progress across various crowdfunding platforms, including Kickstarter, PledgeMusic, and Indiegogo. The series also contains interviews with famous musicians, platform heads, and Berklee Online teachers, as well as me. online.berklee.edu/takenote/roaring-crowdfund/

Max Temkin's Kickstarter FAQ. Max has raised so much money on Kickstarter for his card game Cards Against Humanity and a bunch of other things. His snarky FAQ was the first Kickstarter resource I found helpful when planning my own project. maxistentialism.com/FAQ/#Kickstarter

Marian Call's Blog. Marian Call is the queen of indie artists. She made a comprehensive postmortem on Kickstarter challenges, including budgets and spreadsheets you can use. mariancall.com/Kickstarter-math-is-weird/

Work Made for Hire. Katie Lane gives negotiating and legal advice for freelancers.
www.workmadeforhire.net/

The DIY Musician Blog. CD Baby's DIY musician blog is a varied repository of advice and news for independent artists.
diymusician.cdbaby.com

Hypebot. Hypebot contains all kinds of news and is a great way to stay up on what's happening in the world of indie music and making your own career.
www.hypebot.com

INDEX

photo by Kim Newmoney

Laser Malena-Webber is the singer, guitarist, and one-person management team for the Doubleclicks, an internationally touring band with five albums (three of which charted on *Billboard*), several viral music videos, and over $350,000 raised in Patreon and Kickstarter campaigns since 2014. Laser is the founder of Doubleclicks Records, a label that helps artists leverage the Internet for their careers, and Laser's crowdfunding consulting business, Laser Campaigns, is one of only twenty companies officially endorsed by Kickstarter.

Laser resides in Los Angeles with their talented game-designer husband Richard and cat Marzipan, who is a very good cat.